your life
fantastic

STUBLEY HALL

the speakmans

your life
can be
fantastic
too!

*Life coaches to the rich and famous,
the Speakmans will help you realise
the life and success you richly deserve*

GOLDWING
publishing ltd

Nik and Eva Speakman are represented by
Sue Rider Management.
www.sueridermanagement.co.uk

ISBN: 9780979396502

Distributed by Gazelle Book Services
Tel: +44 (0)152468765
Email: Sales@gazellebooks.co.uk
www.gazellebooks.co.uk

 Printed on paper from renewable sources

GOLDWING
publishing ltd

Contents

Introduction

Welcome to a life coaching book less ordinary!

There are thousands of self help books out there. We know, because we have read most of them! Some are fantastic, some are great and some seem to have been written just for the sake of it. To date, we have spent a combined 37 years studying how it is possible to make your life better. This is not just our profession, it's our passion! Having read the books, practiced the theories ourselves (and developed new ones) and having been fortunate enough to work with thousands of fantastic people over the years, we have put this book together to include the stuff that really works.

We regularly use these techniques in our own lives and more importantly, when coaching others each and every day. There are many therapies out there that might not have been included. That's because we have only selected the ones that seem to get great results every time (as opposed to those that only work some of the time). Indeed, our methods are so effective that we help people break life-long hang ups, phobias and habits usually within just one or two sessions. As a husband and wife life coaching team, not only are we able to provide the benefit of the male and female viewpoint, but we are also able to consult with each other and combine our viewpoints to find the best way of tackling whatever problems are brought to us.

The Speakmans (from l to r) Olivia(10), Nik, Hunter (2) and Eva

Following the huge success of our TV series A LIFE COACH LESS ORDINARY we have been inundated with requests from people around the world who want to be liberated from their personal demons. They have seen us help clients beat food and drink addictions and eliminate the phobias that are crippling their lives. They have seen that in a world where cynicism and bitterness seem to be the norm, we refuse to let negative beliefs determine the direction in which we are going. We eat well and look after our bodies and have tremendous respect for this amazing thing called LIFE. We are successful personally, professionally, spiritually and materially.

But believe us, things weren't always like this. We have consciously made it happen and YOU CAN TOO! Which brings us to the main point of our book. People keep coming up to us and asking "what's your secret?" as if there is some magic pill that we take every day that keeps us upbeat and bursting with vitality. Or they look at our beautiful house and fabulous lifestyle and say, "Oh you're so lucky." Well we can tell you right now that we don't have any magic pills or potions, and as for luck well, that's all about creating your own. We have simply made some basic changes to the way we think and live our lives; changes that we are going to tell you about.

Okay, already you think we are talking about hard work. Yes we are, but the effort we are referring to here is not physical. Sweat is not involved (that's a subject for a whole different book). We are talking about the mental effort that is needed to kick out bad thinking habits and replace them with good ones. Some clients we see are being held hostage in psychological torture chambers where they beat themselves up daily with memories from the past. A few years of this and it's not surprising that they feel worthless and have zero self confidence. To mask their problems, they might go on to develop addictions to smoking, drinking, drugs, gambling or shopping, as you may have seen in our TV series. Eventually they reach a tipping point and tell themselves "I just can't live like this any more." When they come to see us they want to do something about it, but just don't know where to start. This book can be YOUR starting point. As we always say, "ANYTHING IS POSSIBLE!" and it truly is.

Living with a negative inner voice is a bit like being married to a rude, demanding and critical partner. Although the marriage generally makes you feel pretty dispirited and hopeless most of the time, it's kind of secure; everything's familiar and no effort is required. Plus, it has its odd moments when things don't seem so bad. We are here to tell you that you can get divorced from destructive thinking habits and find yourself a nicer inner voice: one that encourages you to look after yourself and treats you with respect. We know, because we have done it ourselves. That's why opening this book will be a bit like opening the door to our lives. We're going to tell you a bit more about ourselves, tell you who has inspired us, show you around our home and let you in on a few of our secrets.

One of our discoveries is the basic law of nature, which is that any living thing must be nurtured to grow or it will wither and die. Growth is life and without the correct mental stimulation and nutrition, you will invariably die. Unfortunately, as a human race we are often brain washed into believing that life is basically a miserable experience and that cynicism and negativity is normal. We have sometimes been called crazy, "daftly naïve," self indulgent or selfish because we prefer to embrace the good things that life has to offer. Don't we watch TV or read the newspapers? The world is full of death and disaster. How can we be happy about anything? Some people say that positive thinking is just a way to shield yourself from reality. In fact, nothing could be further from the truth.

In the following pages we will explain why, in today's increasingly dark and chaotic world, it is so important to resist negativity and pessimism and to identify and realise your dreams, for your own good and for that of those closest to you. It may mean standing up to your inner voice or confronting habits so ingrained that you never realised the harm they were inflicting on yourself and others.

You may ask, "But how is a book going to help me?" The answer is simple. The words in this book will help you to grow. Whatever it is that is stopping you from being the person you want to be: more confident, more successful, less blaming, more relaxed, less fearful...we will help you to identify it and inspire you to begin making changes. It was reading books that made us grow, flourish and blossom each and every day. It is now our ultimate goal to scatter our knowledge to you like petals blowing in the wind...

We are sincerely grateful that you have chosen to read this book and respect you greatly for wanting more from your life than just acceptance of the so-called norm. You can be anything you want to be, so please read on and allow us to share with you the many wonderful things that we have discovered!

We hope that you will enjoy collecting the petals and keep them as sweet smelling pot pourri that freshens your life each and every day for the rest of your FANTASTIC life!

Before you read this book...

Whenever we read a book we just want to get stuck in and discover all the information as soon as we can so we can start trying it out. Maybe you are like that too. But to get the maximum benefit possible and start to see the changes in your life that you want, please consider the following points before carrying on.

1. Know your outcome

We want you to have the life you have always dreamt of. We know that it is possible because we have done it ourselves. As you read on you will find that our story is probably no different from yours in many ways. So PLEASE make the decision not to just accept your life the way it is and not to just settle for anything less than the best that you can possibly be!

Ask yourself why you bought this book. What is it in your life that you want to improve? What is you desired outcome? The more clarity you have the better results you will get. Spend time thinking about the results you want and write them here:

....

....

....

....

2. Make a decision

Totally accept that the above outcome is your main reason for reading this book. Every time you pick up this book, refresh your memory as to why you are reading it. Please also decide that you will not just read it but that you will also work on, and experience all the exercises time and time again, and that you will also follow our guidance that will help you reprogram yourself for success.

3. Take control

If you leave things to chance you are always at the mercy of your surroundings and as Forrest Gump's mother said, "Life is like a box of chocolates, you never know what you are going to get." Quite frankly, if you sit around waiting for life to run you, Mrs. Gump was right! But we want you to start running your own life as you want it. So from now on you will know exactly what you are going to get. If life is like a box of chocolates, let's make sure you design your own box and fill it with amazing flavours and textures. You should make your life so exciting that you go to bed late and get up early and have so much passion for living that you just have to share it with others before you explode!

9

We see this book as the key to your new life in two ways. Firstly, the exercises have been tried, tested and used successfully by both of us and they have changed our lives from a mediocre existence (although looking back at the time we believed it to be great) to the fantastic one we have today.

So it is important that you not only complete each and every one of the exercises, but that you also ask yourself the question, "How can I use this technique in my life?" The exercises *work* and are fantastic, but they will work differently for different people who want different things. By knowing your outcome then asking yourself, "How can I use this technique in my life, to obtain the outcome that I want?" you can focus your mind to your desired outcome.

Secondly, this book must become your key to study as we do not want you to leave anything to chance. We want you to design for yourself the most incredible life possible. Yes, it does involve further studying, but studying of the most fantastic sort. Basically, if you want the best relationship possible, then you have to study relationships. If you want the best healthy eating program possible, you need to study nutrition. If you desire the best body possible, then you must study exercise and so on. When you study from the position of drive and passion towards a desired outcome that will benefit you greatly, it is nothing less than exciting!

Yes we know what you are thinking here, STUDY!!? And yes we understand exactly what your brain is saying, "Oh please no, that is pain!"' That's right, most people associate study with pain. We understand that because the last time you may have studied was at school and you were studying subjects because you had to, not because you wanted to. Furthermore, they were probably not the most exciting subjects either! And that is the difference. When you enjoy learning about a subject that excites you, it comes so naturally that you *want* to do it and you retain more. We are so lucky to live in the age of information and with the Internet it has never been easier to find information on anything that you want to study. In our early days of investigating mind programming, we remember having to order books from the USA via a

bookshop in Manchester and sometimes they would take months to arrive. Fortunately, with companies like Amazon you can now get everything you need far more quickly and easily.

There is also another fantastic shortcut to getting what you want and saving yourself years and years of trying stuff, making mistakes and attempting to reinvent the wheel on the subjects you have chosen. *Find someone else who has done it already.* Sounds simple. Well it is! Sometimes the things that we see as being so simple we just seem to overlook. So if you want the best relationship ever, then don't just study relationships, study ones that have the qualities that you are looking for. For example, don't take advice from your mate who may be on their second marriage. Ask someone who has been married for 40 years and is still madly in love. If you have put weight on and want to lose weight, don't consult someone who has always been overweight or yo-yos up and down. Find someone who was like you: put the weight on, lost it, but also successfully managed to keep it off too. If you find out how they did it and do *exactly* what they did, you will get the same results.

We have huge respect for you for wanting to make a change, for spending your money to purchase this book and most of all for giving your valuable time to read it. Time is the universal currency and therefore should never be wasted. So please, please, please, don't just *read* this book. Practice the exercises, make the changes and if you're in a rut, get out of it. After all, the only difference between a rut and a grave is the depth!

Please appreciate that this is also more than just a book; it is the key or a catalyst to your better future. If you use it correctly it will not only open your mind to new and exciting possibilities; it will also open the door to a library of information and discovery that will enable you to achieve all the outcomes that you desire.

Offering you the utmost respect and encouragement for all that you truly deserve.

1.

Who we are and what we do

I WANTED TO BE AN ASTRONAUT OR A ZOO KEEPER!

Nik Speakman

I still chuckle inside when people say to me, "It's OK for you; you can be so positive because you have got everything you need. You don't know what it is like to have to struggle all your life you're lucky." Yes, in many ways I have been very lucky. I had loving parents who adored me and looked after me brilliantly. Their relationship was strong and mutually supportive and they were married for 53 years until my father passed away in 2001. So yes, I was very lucky in that respect. Family life was great and I look back with fondness and appreciation for what should be considered a normal upbringing, but sadly seems quite a rarity these days.

This is me, aged 13

My father was a mill worker who started work at 13 years of age. By attending night school and studying hard he progressed to the position of mill manager, achieving well over 50 years' service with the same employer. My parents raised my older brother and me in a modest two-bedroom terraced house in the town of Royton in the North of England. My father earned a reasonable wage, certainly enough to make sure we never went short; however, he could never really afford to be extravagant.

Even so, my dad was (and still is) one of the happiest people I have ever known. I now realise that he had discovered the secret of

What drove me?..... Ferraris!!!

NIC SP

life: ultimate fulfillment. For him, that was a wife and family he loved, a job so close to home he could have lunch with his family and a house that backed out onto the local park. (He used to joke that he had the biggest garden in Royton!)

Until the age of 16, I went to an all boys' grammar school where I excelled despite the fact I was there only about 60% of the time as I was absent a lot through sickness. As early as I can remember, I suffered from severe eczema and I used to go to bed creamed and bandaged like an Egyptian mummy and wearing mitts to prevent myself from scratching. As I reached about six years-old, the eczema began to improve, but I developed asthma so badly that I was hospitalised on several occasions. I was on all kinds of steroid medications, various injections (I still don't know what they were for) and antibiotics; I became very pale and thin. For years I was medically supervised and attended hospital on a monthly basis to be weighed and measured as I was simply not growing. At school, I was the kid who wasn't there that much and being different I soon became bullied.

This bullying carried on until one day I remember thinking, "I've had enough of this" and hit one of my attackers back. I got a major beating in return, but undeterred I did this twice more until I was left alone. I realised soon after that it was easier for bullies to pick on someone who didn't respond; like vultures they always want easy prey. This was a turning point in my life because I vowed I would make myself fitter and stronger so I would never be in that situation again and I would be able to assist anyone else who was a victim of bullying.

My dad was always exercising because of his interest in bodybuilding or "physical culture" as it was called in those days, so there were weights and exercise equipment around the house. This was definitely a big influence on me. But quite literally the biggest influence was Arnold Schwarzenegger who became my first role model. This was back in 1977, when he was in the UK promoting his new film *Pumping Iron*. He was being interviewed on the *Russell Harty Show* and I was completely blown away by his awesome size and how amazing he looked. He made me realise that we are not governed by anything, including the body we were

Follow Your Dreams

"Determination gives you the drive to crash through any road blocks that may lie ahead."

Nik Speakman

15

Left: Arnie is my hero. From being the son of a poor Austrian military officer he became the greatest bodybuilder of the 20th century, an International superstar and is now the Governor of California. Arnold is living proof that "Anything Is Possible." So if he wants it, I would bet that even the American constitution could be changed to allow him to become the next US President!

born with and if we choose to do so then we can even defy nature. I thought, "I want that." So the combination of never wanting to be bullied again and being focused on emulating this amazing man drove me on to weight train regularly ever since.

Another passion of mine that I had from a very early age was a love of cars, Ferraris and Lamborghinis in particular. As a boy of 7, I remember asking my dad why he didn't own a Ferrari and he told me that he didn't want one. I just couldn't understand it! How could anyone NOT want a Ferrari? I was really confused as I had no idea about this ultimate fulfillment thing he had going on.

For my eighth birthday I asked for a camera so I could go out in search of Ferraris and other sports cars and take photos and see them "in the metal" so to speak. It was far more exciting than looking at pictures in a book. I could touch them and imagine what it would be like to drive one. For years I took photos of every super car I could find and accumulated pictures of every vehicle worth owning. The only one that eluded me was my ultimate super car, the Lamborghini Countach.

One day, an amazing thing happened. While taking a photograph of a Ferrari 400GT the owner walked by. We not only chatted for ages but he took me for my first ride in a Ferrari! I will never forget that, it was awesome, I wanted one. It was another life changing moment. Suddenly, the photographs had some reality. From that day on, I promised myself that whatever it took I was going to own exotic cars. This passion became a motivating force in my life. In fact, the cars have quite literally driven me.

Against the odds (with my poor school attendance record due to ill health) I still managed to do well at school. So when I saw the school's careers advisor, he probably expected me to say I wanted to be a doctor or a lawyer. I remember sitting there as he asked, "Well Speakman, what do you want to do?" "Sir, I want to be an astronaut." There was a long silence before he replied sarcastically, "Speakman, both you and I know there are no space programs in the UK, so that's a non-starter. What else do you want to do?" As I loved animals, I then suggested zookeeper. The teacher said, "Speakman be serious. The nearest zoo is Chester (about 60 miles away). How are you going to get there every day? Besides, that job is not just about having fun and looking at nice animals, there will be a lot of cleaning to do. Have you thought of that?" As pitiful as it was, that was the full extent of my careers advice. Talk about shattering your dreams!

My career path was actually a little more conventional as it turned out. After obtaining the necessary qualifications and experience while working for a bank and a finance company I qualified as a financial adviser. I was really pushing things with my bodybuilding and most surprisingly to me, as I considered myself now to be very fit, I became very ill again and was hospitalised for three weeks. I was diagnosed with a severe case of ulcerative colitis, which I was informed was incurable. I was told that if the condition stabilised I may be able to keep it under control by taking medication for the rest of my life. However, if the disease didn't stay in remission the ulcerated part of my colon would have to be removed and during the operation the surgeon would assess whether I would be left with enough colon to function normally or whether he would have to remove it altogether and fit a colostomy bag. What a wake up call!

I made a decision there and then, that no one was going to cut me open. In the short term I took the medication religiously while I found out as much as I could about my condition. I eventually discovered that my problems were caused by a combination of over-prescribed antibiotics as a child which had not only killed whatever infection I had at the time but had also destroyed all the good bacteria that is required for a healthy colon. I had also been following a so-called healthy bodybuilder's diet from my late teens, which I now know was totally incorrect for my body's chemical make up. The bodybuilder diet consisted of a large amount of milk and egg protein. The great news is that I am now able to control my condition with healthy eating, Swamp Joose® and exercise and all WITHOUT the use of drugs. (And yes, I still have my colon fully intact!)

Being hospitalised, facing time off work, and not wanting to relive my school days, I decided to set up my own business. I had no idea how to start or become successful, so I began looking for answers. First, I asked an accountant for advice. Then I came across my first self help books: *The Structure of Magic* by Richard Bandler and John Grinder and *Unlimited Power* by Anthony Robbins. After reading these books and subsequently many others, my initial reaction was, "If this stuff is so easy then surely everyone would be doing it." But my defining moment was when I attended a seminar by Robin Fielder entitled *Close That Sale*. All the delegates were given a work book and Robin said, "Before you open your workbook, write on the front **OPEN YOUR MIND**." I pretty much missed the whole seminar because of that one statement. My thoughts wandered and I spent the whole time mulling

17

over his words. What did he mean? Why would anyone close their mind? How could that be possible? What was he talking about? This really got me thinking about new possibilities and searching for more answers.

In 1986, I did indeed set up my own business as a financial adviser. It began to grow slowly but surely. I also became involved in estate agency and things started to get even better. In fact, everything was going successfully except my personal life. I now know

This was quite literally the wedding that I had dreamed of! I married Eva in 1996 on the beach at Sanibel, Florida.

that what you focus on is exactly what you get. As I had spent so much time focusing on my business and had neglected my relationship with a long time girlfriend, we had grown apart. This then resulted in us making each other unhappy and staying together for all the wrong reasons.

I loved America and Florida in particular as I had vacationed there many times. During one visit I decided to go back and study for my Florida Real Estate License. When my relationship was over I thought about going to Florida as an escape and possibly combining selling houses with a financial business. By this time, I had qualified as an estate agent on both sides of the ocean. Then my world suddenly changed. I met Eva the very day before I was due to go to the USA to discuss some of the fantastic business opportunities that were being created because of the growing market of Brits looking for second homes.

But while in Florida, I could not stop thinking about the gorgeous little blonde sales rep who had visited my office in England. During that three-week trip, I spent a lot of time on my own and I remember sitting on a beach in Sanibel one evening, with my mind on Eva and suddenly thought, "When I get married I would like it to be here." Up to that point I had never thought about marriage at all. Yet this is exactly where Eva and I did eventually marry five years later, on that very same beach. What an amazing example of the power of visualisation!

"Life is basically the same for everyone. Good and bad things happen to us all and whatever occupies our thoughts we feel. The key to life then surely is being able to manage not our lives but our thoughts."

Nik Speakman

"Once you say you can't, you shut the door. If you say you can (even if you don't know how), you open your mind and eyes to infinite possibilities to make it happen."

Nik Speakman

You might be thinking, yes but where does the life coaching come in? As I have reflected back on my life I now realise that I have been coaching people throughout my career. All the time I was giving financial advice I was thinking about my client's future in the long term. It wasn't just about getting them to sign up for the latest tax saving scheme or finding the best mortgage deal. The same thing applied when I was selling houses. I wanted the best for the people who came to see me and advised them to invest in the most expensive house they could afford, get the maximum mortgage they could get, live in the house a couple of years then sell it and do the same again until they had acquired the house they really wanted (which was against the grain of thinking at the time). Any houses prior to that were merely stepping stones. Not everyone took this advice, but the ones who did are very comfortably off and all own the houses that they always wanted all those years ago!

I was always very interested in helping people and I now recognise and firmly believe, that this is the main reason why I was put on this earth. Since reading my first self improvement books in 1986, my knowledge has escalated and grown as the more I discover about the human capabilities the more I wish know. And the more I discover, the more I can share with others. I have now had the benefit of reading hundreds of books relating to self improvement, motivation and psychology. I have attended many seminars and been fortunate enough to have received training from some of the best people in the world in their fields.

That said, I am still looking for answers and I

With Scott Wright in 2006

continue daily on my quest looking for new and exciting ideas that will enable us to assist people change for the better, more quickly and easily than ever before. Eva and I still read at an absolute minimum of one new book every month and we try and attend as many seminars and training courses as we can. In fact, we have attended some of them time and again as we firmly believe that repetition is the mother of skill. Like watching your favourite movie repeatedly, there are always new things you notice. Plus we are reminded of great things that we already know but may have forgotten to use.

I have also realised that it *is* possible for people to close their minds. In fact they are more often closed than open! Practicing the art of having an open mind doesn't come easily, but when you do it numerous possibilities open up and things really do start falling into place. My initial skepticism disappeared when I accepted this. Then I looked back at my life and saw that on an unconscious level I had been practicing the stuff myself and furthermore it had worked like magic!

With our combined knowledge, training and experience, Eva and I have discovered that we are able to turn people's lives around by tuning in to their problems, fixing them and pointing them in the right direction. The rewards I gain from seeing such big changes in people is just so incredible. Nothing can beat it. I realise that this was the reason why I was put on this earth. It was my passion and my destiny. I therefore embraced it with both arms and shouted, "**World I'm Here!**" And that, as they say, is how it all began!

"𝔑ik and 𝔈va must be the best life coaches in the world."

𝔖cott 𝔚right (𝔗𝔙 and film actor)

Inspiring lives...

There are many great men and women who have shaped the way millions of people think and have brought about real change to the world. One person can make all this possible, purely through the power of their self-belief and extreme focus. When you think of the struggles and the ridicule that these powerfully influential characters have overcome, it is even more impressive.

The people that are featured in these pages have made a huge impact on both Eva and I, and still inspire us today. They represent all that is positive, energetic and GREAT in the true sense of the word. Human beings have so much to offer the world, but most make very little impression upon it. What makes all these role models so different and why did they succeed? I have read so many books about courageous and independent-spirited men and women throughout history, but the few I have chosen here are, in my eyes, outstanding beyond belief and all possess a totally unique kind of courage.

Mahatma Gandhi (1869 – 1948)

Mahatma Gandhi

We have a picture of Mahatma Gandhi in our treatment room. It is hard to believe that this thoughtful and unassuming man would become a major political and spiritual leader of the Indian independence movement. As a pioneer of mass non-violent resistance, his teachings inspired civil rights leaders such as Dr Martin Luther King Jr., Steve Biko and Nelson Mandela.

Gandhi helped poor farm workers protest against discrimination, worked for the liberation of women and for an end to social discrimination and poverty. As a student of the Hindu philosophy he lived very simply, making his own clothes and living on a strict vegetarian diet. This amazing man lived an incredible life and will always be remembered for the courage and hope he inspired in others.

21

Steve Irwin (1962 – 2006)

"I'm like the boy who never grew up. I'm very, very passionate about what I do. I mean, I love what I do. I wake up in the morning on fire..."

Steve Irwin

Steve Irwin

Eva and I were deeply saddened to hear about the death of the Australian wildlife warrior, conservationist and crocodile hunter Steve Irwin in September 2006. His zest for life, generosity and immense courage were just some of the characteristics of this unique man. He educated millions, teaching people about some of the most unloved creatures in nature: the reptiles and crocodiles that people wanted to kill.

For me, Steve was the ultimate in zoo keepers as he also had a bit of Tarzan and Dr Doolittle in him too. I just loved watching him so much more than I had done Johnny Morris, David Bellamy and David Attenborough before him. He was so enthusiastic and passionate; what a fantastic role model Steve was to anyone who worked at a zoo or anyone like me who had desires of being a zoo keeper.

Through his work with the Australia Zoo, his legacy to protect these animals will always live on. Steve also founded Wildlife Warriors Worldwide to protect the habitats of endangered species. It is not generally known, but he also purchased large areas of land throughout Australia and the rest of the world, to preserve them as wildlife habitat.

Steve and his family lived modestly, using their wealth to support programs to help protect defence-less wild animals whose lives are under threat. His enthusiasm and passion for everything he did endeared him to millions around the world. He never lost the spirit and wonderment of his youth and had the kind of infectious energy that makes the world a better and brighter place.

Frank Kaczka

Frank Kazka is a great friend and inspiration

An inspiration to both Eva and I, is our dear friend Frank who we met in Florida in 1993. When we first encountered Frank we saw a handsome, toned, interesting and intelligent young man. All Frank could see was that he was a disabled wheelchair-bound cripple. He was angry... very angry. He was bitter and engulfed in a rage of revenge. His words of anger, justifiable self pity and hatred made him ugly and unpleasant.

From being a very fit and hugely muscular fitness trainer who was extremely popular with the girls, Frank was now paralysed from the chest down. While working as a doorman outside a nightclub in Hawaii in his early 20s, he was shot by an insanely jealous client who had developed a crush on him. As he lay dying on the ground, his lungs filling with blood, his attacker laughed with satisfaction. The gunman was jailed and later died in prison. But Frank found it very difficult to come to terms with his disability and the fact that his attacker had escaped by dying while he had to live with his physical handicap permanently. But slowly over the days, months and years, Frank transformed into a tremendous, awesome and inspiring man. He made the decision that he was not a cripple and would not be treated as such. He wanted to live independently and would not even have a handicapped car.

The first time I saw him drive I was amazed. He had a Ford Thunderbird, a real muscle car! He maneuvered himself alongside the driver's door, tilted his wheelchair onto one wheel and unclipped the other, which he put onto the rear seat. He then lifted himself out of the wheelchair and into the driver's seat. Once in the car, he leant out and picked up the wheelchair with one hand, swung it round and put that on the rear seat too. Awesome!

He knows that he will walk again one day and that modern science will enable him to do so. He is totally self-sufficient, works as a personal trainer and gym instructor and continues to train and looks fantastic. As a mentor to young people wishing to become body builders and power lifters he is a remarkable and true inspiration. (Some of his hard-earned motivational words are, "You are working harder now than anyone else in this gym and I am proud of you for that!") We were so thrilled that Frank agreed to be my best man when we were married on Sanibel Island in Florida.

On the rare occasion that I have a day when I think I can't do something or feel a little under the weather, I think of Frank and the daily challenges he has to conquer. That always puts my life into perspective and gets me off my behind and taking action in no time!

Arnold Schwarzenegger: The embodiment of success

Before he became a huge box-office success, Arnold Schwarzenegger was THE name in bodybuilding. He was Mr. Universe five times and Mr. Olympia seven times and as one of the most influential figures in the bodybuilding community he certainly made a massive impression on me in my youth. In my eyes, he is one of the greatest men alive and has overcome so many barriers purely with the strength of his indomitable spirit. As he says, "The

secret is to make your mind work for you – not against you."

I have followed him for almost 30 years and he is a true inspiration to me. As I have discovered, success leaves clues, and therefore it is important to have role models, as they can make the mistakes for you so you can avoid them, they can then show you their formulas to success. Arnie has done so many things that people just don't know about. His life has not always been great and he has not always been so physically robust, in addition, he literally started with nothing.

Just as Arnie was my role model, as a teenager, *his* role model was the champion American body builder Reg Park. Arnold idolised him. Referring to him as "pure inspiration" he moulded himself on his hero. Reg had plenty of cash, he was a successful movie actor and he lived in the USA. This became everything that Arnold dreamed of for himself.

In 1966, he entered Mr. Europe contest and won. Then in 1967 he finally met his "fantasy father figure" Reg Park. When Reg would train, Arnold would copy his every move and learn everything he could to follow in his footsteps. Later that year, Arnold won Mr. Universe, but he was furious when he discovered there were other Mr. Universe titles to be won, depending on which federation had organised the competition. He became even more obsessed with being number one.

In 1968, he won his second Mr. Universe competition and met the legendary body builder Joe Weider who encouraged him to go to the United States. Arnold arrived in the USA with just $10 in his pocket and moved to Santa Monica where he continued to work out in the gym and on Venice Beach. At the age of 23, he became Mr. Universe again and four weeks later picked up the title of Mr. Olympia. After this, he toured the world in posing exhibitions. Deciding that it was time to make some serious money, he set up a construction business with a long time friend. It was extremely successful owing to the number of earthquakes in the area! Arnold was soon making thousands of dollars and for the first time money was not a worry in his life. (Let me say here and now Arnold wasn't "lucky" in any of this. He had goals, drive and ambition, he was willing to put the effort in and create his own luck, just as Eva and I do.)

Arnold persisted with his dream of becoming a movie star like Reg Park. He contacted several film producers, but the reaction was always the same: "Your name is strange, your body is strange, your accent is strange... Go on, beat it!" But as a fellow actor said of him, "Arnold welcomed a challenge. It motivated him even more when he was told that he couldn't do something."

His first acting role was in a film called *Hercules in New York*, although he was credited as Arnold Strong as the directors said no one would remember the name Arnold Schwarzenegger. (How wrong they were!) They also decided to dub his voice because they thought his accent was too thick. Eventually he appeared under his own name in a film called *Stay Hungry* which earned him good reviews and a Golden Globe for Most Promising Actor.

Arnold starred in many films such as *Conan the Barbarian, Red Sonya and Conan the Destroyer* and they were all a great success. Next came *The Terminator* (although he nearly didn't get the lead because the director didn't think he would be able to say the lines properly). *The Terminator* launched Arnold's movie career into the stratosphere!

In 1986, after dating for nine years, Arnold married Maria Shriver, despite their conflicting political views. (Arnold was a Republican and Maria's background was Democrat.) Two more movie successes followed with *Commando* and *Predator*. Then in 1988, Arnold signed to do the movie *Twins* with Danny DeVito. Again he was faced with doubts about his abilities, so much so that Universal Studios offered only to pay him if the film made money. *Twins* grossed $100 million and Arnold received $30 million.

That same year, Arnold's next movie, *Total Recall* generated $261 million worldwide. Then the massively popular and long awaited, *Terminator 2*, grossed half a billion dollars! He was officially the biggest

"I never met anyone who could focus in the moment NOW the way that Arnold did. It was surreal, almost metaphysical."

Barbara Outland

"Arnie's life story is just like one of his films, with the exception that as unbelievable as it may appear, it is true! Arnie is a real life hero."

Nik Speakman

movie star in the United States and had obliterated his initial goals of just being a successful actor. That is what I love so much about Arnold if he wants to do something he just doesn't just do it; no that is never enough. He becomes the best!

His political career was also blossoming. His support for Proposition 49 to get kids off the street resulted in the bill being passed. Once again, Arnold was a hero. To add to his fortunes, *Terminator 3* was another blockbuster and made him the highest paid movie actor on the planet. In 2003, he ran for Governor of California against 138 other candidates (which included professional politicians, a comedy actor and a porn star!). The seasoned politicians were less than impressed. They could not fathom how someone totally lacking in political or governmental experience could run a state the size of California. Yet Arnold won with 48% of the vote and was the first foreign-born Governor of the State.

The first to call and congratulate him were Nelson Mandela and George Bush. But the first person that Arnold contacted was Reg Park, his all time hero and mentor. Reg reportedly said it would not surprise him if the next time he called it was to say he had got to the White House. (In 2003, when Eva and I were on a TV programme called *That's Rich* I said that if Arnold wanted it badly enough he would get the American constitution changed so that he could become President. I firmly believe that if it is something that Arnie wants, he has the ability and drive to make it happen. So just watch this space!)

Today Arnold is even more successful as a State Governor than body builder or actor. In 2004/5 the California State budget was in a dire state and facing possible bankruptcy. By the time of his 2007/8 budget report, he was forecasting a balanced budget with no deficit

© Karin Lau

Left: Taking oath of office at his inauguration ceremony with First Lady Maria Shriver. Is the White House next?

whatsoever! Arnold is also very active on climate control to curb global warming and is a keen supporter of innovative alternative energy producing technologies.

One of his closest friends explains his extraordinary approach to life, "Arnold has his head in the clouds, but keeps his feet on the ground. This is the key to his success." And this is how one man, who arrived in the States with absolutely nothing except a dream, ended up with absolutely everything.

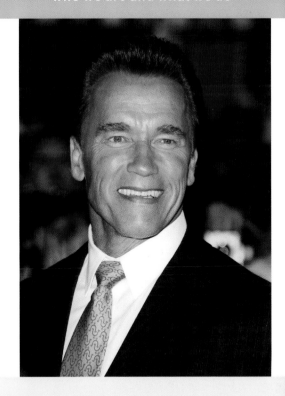

"I've seen first hand coming here with empty pockets but full of dreams, full of desire, full of will to succeed, but with the opportunities that I had, I could make it."

"For me life is continuously being hungry. The meaning of life is not simply to exist, to survive, but to move ahead, to go up, to achieve, to conquer."

"The resistance that you fight physically in the gym and the resistance that you fight in life can only build a strong character."

"The mind is the limit. As long as the mind can envision the fact that you can do something, you can do it, as long as you really believe one hundred percent."

HAVING MY CAR STOLEN WAS THE BEST THING THAT EVER HAPPENED TO ME!

Eva Speakman

Like Nik, I was very well provided for. My parents were very generous and I wanted for nothing. I was the youngest and was without doubt spoiled. Being spoiled was compounded by the fact that I was a sickly child and suffered with eczema. Then at the age of 6, I developed kidney failure and spent many weeks in hospital and many months out of school.

We always had a warm home, delicious food (as my mum was a spectacular cook) clothes, toys and plenty of pocket money. I spoke very little English when I started school as our first language was Polish, therefore I was never considered one of the brightest at junior school and I often lagged behind. My dad was keen on us being well educated so I was sent to an all girls private Catholic convent school which was a quiet and lonely existence. In school I was very shy and introverted and was quite a loner, which intensified when my best friend moved away at age 6. I spent most play times alone with my great imagination. A tree in the playground would transform into a rocket and provided many happy hours of make believe as it would take me to lands made of candy with lemonade rivers and chocolate trees!

Although my parents loved one another, they had a very volatile relationship and shouting and aggression occurred frequently. Their loud arguments pained me greatly throughout my childhood and also made me nervous about inviting friends over as I had portrayed that I came from a peaceful home.

Being of Eastern European descent, alcohol was a major part of our family life. Like a cancer that refused to leave it hung over our home life like a putrid stench of rot. Alcohol was always the instigator of the pain, fear, emotional turmoil and aggression. The great news was that positivity can be extracted from every negative situation and my home life taught me that peace, harmony, love, energy and joy were all "definites" on my life goal list. I learned exactly what I *didn't*

Here I am aged 3

want from my life and I knew without a shadow of a doubt that I would never be a prisoner of alcohol, or any other drug for that matter.

From an early age I knew that I wanted to make a positive difference and to help people, although I was not quite sure how. My childhood ambition was to be a teacher, actress or even a missionary. That last one may sound corny, but it seemed like a great means to not only teach children in a third world, but to utilise my love of theatre by singing and dancing with the children. Plus going to Africa or Papua New Guinea was a great way of escaping at the same time. However, the thought of leaving my mum plus my lack of self confidence prevented me from taking the next step in this area.

Another memorable experience I endured (although I tried to forget it at the time) was the emotional and physical bullying from a close family member. This started when I was teenie weenie and continued into adulthood. I must add that there were good periods and bad and although the physical bullying stopped in my late teens, the emotional bullying continued until Nik helped to give me the strength to slam that door shut and use the experience to help others. Life coaching has taught me that it is totally okay to cut ties with people who hurt you, belittle you, drag you down or make you feel inadequate in any way at all EVEN IF THEY ARE FAMILY. This had always been against my parental conditioning and was thus a very difficult step.

Above: Aged 6 and in my early twenties. Below: This was me in 1993 on holiday with Nik.

Most victims of bullying or domestic violence are kind and benevolent people who wish to see the good in everyone and so they eagerly accept apologies in the belief those things will never happen again. Furthermore, victims are made to feel weak and inadequate and start convincing themselves that they deserve this punishment. However, believe me *no one* deserves to be hurt or belittled emotionally or physically in any way EVER.

Senior school was a huge turning point in my life and was a tremendous experience! My parents had arranged private tuition for me in my latter years of junior school so I had just started to feel academically more confident. The day I walked in to my new senior school, where only two other girls had joined me from my junior school, I decided there and then that I would create the content of the unfolding chapters of my life. I would no longer be seen as the slow one

in lessons, or the shy kid on her own in the playground. This was the day my line of "WORLD I'M HERE" was born!

I was consistently top of the class; I studied hard and achieved. I joined the drama group and choir and was a main character in every school play, musical and pantomime. I was always at my happiest when on the stage or during exams. At these times nothing mattered and I was sitting pretty on top of planet Eva exuding sparkle!

During my senior school years I had great encouragement from a truly magnificent teacher who made an impact on me in more ways than he'll ever know. It was Mr. John Keating, my English and drama teacher who inspired and encouraged me to shine on stage and in class. He made me feel I could do anything with my life. He demonstrated to me and the class, that it was humanly possible to be vibrant, energetic and happy! Also, from being very poor in English, this man helped me to achieve the second highest mark in my English language and English Literature exams.

Mr. Keating was convinced I should be a performer and suggested to my mother that I had professional singing and drama lessons. Although she was flattered to think her daughter might have talent and would often boast about my capabilities, she did not know how to go about finding a professional private tutor. When I told her I wanted to be a TV presenter she was thrilled but would often remind me that it wasn't easy to do, and therefore advised me to stick to being a teacher. When I look back, I realise I have a lot to thank Mr. Keating for because it was his belief in me that has given me the confidence to face the cameras today.

The downside to senior school was that I was bullied by a group of girls who called me fat and ugly and threatened to hurt me on my way home from school. I dreaded that journey. Thankfully, a couple of great school friends and neighbours, Jason and Neil would often walk with me, which unbeknown to them was my ticket home without the fear of a beating. However, this resulted in the bullies labelling me a slut. This was the worst thing anyone could ever say as my moral values were very important to me.

I now know that these bullies were self conscious, idle, self loathing, under achievers, who like every other bully can not stand anyone being above them mentally or physically. A bully would much rather knock other people down to below their level than put the effort in to build themselves up.

It was ironic that on the week the second series of our hit TV show was being aired, I walked through a market and past the leader of this pack of school bullies. She was sitting on a bench wearing the apron and name badge of the local store where she now worked. She had bad posture, bitten finger nails, tatty hair and was dragging on her cigarette like it was the only light in her life. I wonder how much happier she would have been today had she chosen to join me on my trip to achievement as opposed to her chosen pastime of demolishing the confidence of those around her.

After senior school, despite my ambitions to become a missionary or an actress, I decided to listen to my mother and do as she suggested and go to university to study French. But before that, I took a year out to study health and beauty at college for what I thought would be a bit of an academic relief. Instead, I found myself really enjoying the course; so my career goal took a different direction.

To fund my studies I took a part time job at a local estate agency selling houses and arranging mortgages. After a couple of years, (by which time I had got my beauty therapist's diploma) I was head hunted by one of the bank managers who asked me if I would be interested in accepting the position of regional sales representative. It was a fantastic opportunity with a company car and lots of benefits. I knew the position was well above what I was capable of at that actual moment, but I also knew that anything was possible. In fact, at the interview I believed in myself so much that I was able to convey with energy and confidence that I would be a knockout at the job!

My knees momentarily turned to jelly though, when I was given a target in year one of £4 million pounds sterling of mortgage lending. Yet I managed to hit and surpass this and was consequently given a £10 million target in year two and £19 million in year three. All targets were hit and exceeded.

I felt invincible! I had a great job, great income and a great future. I remember telling my then boyfriend with pride and enthusiasm that my goals and dreams were beginning to come true and that by the age of 30 I wouldn't have to work any more unless I wanted to. Big Mistake! He didn't want to grow with me, or with anyone else for that matter. He opted to damage my beautifully forming roots and to smash my dreams by beating me to the point of hospitalisation on more than one occasion. He also offered me constant recitations of how useless and pathetic I was. It's amazing how when you're told something enough times you start to believe it. "You're pathetic... who do you think you are? Your head's in the clouds!" he would shout and rant.

This experience taught me not to expect anyone to understand or support my self belief. It was mine and I had to hold on to it and protect it. I have learnt that people who stamp on your dreams do so because they are inadequate themselves and feel threatened by them. It takes hard work, courage and determination to be successful and they don't want to make the effort. They then have a choice: to attack themselves for being lazy and scared, or to

Together in 1992...

still in love in 1993...

...and in 1994!

attack you for being successful. Of course, they choose the latter! I also became aware that any man that I met would have to share the same kind of self belief and drive. As fate would have it, I was destined to meet my life partner quite soon afterwards.

One day an angel arranged for my car to be stolen on a cold dark winter's evening in a secluded, dark and scary car park. Wow, what a wonderful day that was! My manager was unable to keep a business appointment so I was sent instead to meet financial adviser and business proprietor Nik Speakman. Aged 21, with an array of blonde curls, high heels and briefcase in hand, my first instincts were that Nik was very businesslike and matter of fact. But following lunch I knew I had found a kindred spirit. He had vision and he wanted to help others and he applauded other people's success, which was remarkable. I had only ever come across emotional demolishers, not builders and applauders.

Nik had a vision of the future and not many people have that. After lunch, we went back to his office only to find my car had been stolen. I was mortified. Nik was lovely; he made me sweet tea, reassured me, then called my dad and the police. Even though he was within hours of jetting off to the States (and still hadn't packed), he insisted on driving me home. He was my knight in shining armour. Now I look back and think that having my car stolen was one of the best things that could have happened!

When we did get romantically involved, from the first kiss which was electrifying, I knew I would spend the rest of my life with Nik. We moulded together instantly into one bright and eternal energy. Oddly enough, now we were together, our determination to succeed in life seemed to annoy people even more. Not only did we have successful careers, we also had the most wonderful, mutually respectful and supportive relationship.

We were known as "Paul and Linda" after the McCartneys who had one of the closest partnerships ever. People said we weren't normal because we were so deliriously in love. On the other hand, Nik's friends would say "I'm looking for an Eva," and some of my friends would say, "I'm looking for a Nik." It was good to think that they were inspired by us and saw that it *is* possible to find a true soul mate.

Nik and I lived together for five years and as marriage never seemed necessary it therefore had never crossed my mind. Then one night, after I had fallen asleep following a very late party, Nik woke me up, went down

"The best relationship is when your love for each other exceeds your need for each other."

Eva Speakman

on one knee and proposed armed with a beautiful diamond ring. With my frizzy slept on hair, bad breath and bloodshot eyes I realised this guy must really love me. (But I knew when my car had been stolen it was to make way for cupid who had travelled in on a magnificent chariot with Nik my Prince Charming at the helm!)

We got married when I was 26 and Nik was 33. With our combined experience in finance our businesses were flourishing. At about this time we had also discovered exercising together and had begun looking after ourselves properly. Before I met Nik I had been a heavy smoker, overweight and far from fit. In my younger days I worked in a bar where I would beat the men at the yard of ale drinking competition! But once I had found Nik I stopped smoking completely and changed my diet by cutting out anything acidifying or toxic.

The effects were amazing! I soon had masses of energy, sparks were flying off! I also started exercising and discovered the magic of feeling truly awesomely fit. During my beauty therapy course I had started to work towards qualifications in nutrition and sport. I did this over a three-year period and then continued in America with Nik, thanks to a dear friend in Florida who owned a health club. When we returned to the UK we decided to branch out and open a health club ourselves in a derelict church that we converted.

As life coaches we are living proof that the power of belief, the magic of goal setting and pure determination can take you anywhere you want to go. Despite the problems we suffered when we were younger, despite our unhealthy lifestyles and despite our severe illnesses, we have totally redesigned the way we live, the way we look and how we feel. All we did was write down a list of goals, make up our minds why they were important to us and then worked out how we could achieve them.

Now Nik and I live in what I can only describe as the house of our dreams. We have two fantastic, beautiful children, Olivia and Hunter, and can afford to treat ourselves to the finer things in life (for me, that's designer shoes and for Nik it's exotic cars!) Best of all, we've got the most fantastic, brilliant, amazing job in the world; we help people find their dreams and get rid of all the psychological obstacles that are tripping them up and getting in their way.

Every day clients come to us and open up their hearts in a way they may never do even with members of their own family. Such trust is not given lightly and we respect and appreciate everyone who comes to us for help. For me, it's often very emotional to see the difference in someone who comes in burdened by problems and leaves feeling lightened and positive with a great big smile on their face! There is no better job than changing people's lives and we are so proud and privileged to have been given that opportunity. It is also gratifying to know that my personal adversities can be used to strengthen and heal others.

Although I had a lot of love and many happy times during childhood and I was materially blessed, domestic violence, people very close to me breaking the law and being imprisoned, alcoholism, violence, bullying, rape, and sexual abuse have all played a part in my life. I am not sharing this with you now to gain sympathy as I am totally okay with everything. My only reason for sharing this is to emphasise that NOTHING should hold you back; THE PAST IS HISTORY. I hope to be a living example of the theory that *anything really is possible* no matter what adversities stand in your way.

Inspiring lives...

I know the importance of having role models and of emulating people who bravely overcome immense personal challenges and who make a real difference in the world. These people have impressed me greatly and I would like to share the reasons why.

My Mother

I greatly love and respect my mum who was adopted when she was young and was then cruelly abused. Despite a lifetime of aggression and bullying she found the strength, motivation and energy at the age of 55 to think of herself and take control. For the first time ever she has a career at which she has excelled, a harmonious relationship and she has discovered the meaning of home and peace.

My Grandfather

My grandfather George Bielski is a phenomenal man. My mother only rediscovered him 20 years ago. He now lives in Australia and is married to a remarkable lady named Joan, who was awarded the "Order of Australia" (equivalent to a British OBE) for her efforts in Women's Education.

My grandfather George watched his mother beaten, mutilated and burnt alive and lost his father and sister at the hands of the Nazis. At 23 he was placed on death row in the concentration camp at Auschwitz, but he made the decision to live and managed through tact and determination to befriend the Nazis which enabled him to survive.

After the war, despite being shot and hunted by the Nazis and having to change his name, my grandfather was one of the key witnesses at the Nuremberg trials which successfully convicted many of the Gestapo's leaders. His strength of spirit, immense wisdom, determination and will to live is awe inspiring.

Linda Hamilton

I first saw Linda Hamilton in the movie *Terminator*. Yet when I saw her again in *Terminator 2* she had the most amazing arm and shoulder definition. Wow, what a transformation! I vowed at that moment that I would develop the same physique. I soon realised how much effort she had put in to get into shape for the film, as I put myself through exactly the same routine. But I also got the same results!

Gail Devers

The story of the American sprinter Gail Devers is an account of one of the most incredible comebacks in sports history. Not only did she overcome a severe illness that could have incapacitated her for the rest of her life, but she built herself back up again to be one of the most successful sprinters ever. Gail reminds me of a female version of Nik's hero Lance Armstrong.

She was the fastest woman in the world after winning the 100m sprint in the 1992 Olympics. But just four years earlier, Gail had been diagnosed with a condition whose treatment almost resulted in her feet being amputated. Her problems began in 1988 when she was competing in trials for the Olympics in Seoul. She was running poorly, but more worryingly, her hair had started to fall out, a large goiter then appeared on her neck and she would lose vision in one eye for hours at a time.

Gail was diagnosed as having Grave's disease which is a chronic thyroid condition. There were drugs that she could have taken to control the symptoms, but unfortunately they were classed as banned substances by the US Olympic Committee. So she opted for radiation therapy which had severe side effects, one of which was that it caused her feet to swell up dramatically. She literally had to crawl from her bed to the bathroom because the skin on her swollen feet was cracked and bleeding so badly. Amazingly, despite her terrible predicament, she still thought that hope was on the horizon saying, "I knew that if I could weather the storm then the sun was going to shine again." That is such an amazing statement that I have thought about during difficult times in my life.

Just two days before her feet were due to be amputated, the doctors realised that the radiation treatments were causing her problems and changed her treatment.

Gradually she was able to walk again and eventually put her running shoes back on. After just 17 months of rehabilitation and training Gail reached such a peak of fitness that she won a gold medal at the Olympics in Barcelona. She then continued to be the best sprinter in both indoor and outdoor competition and became only the second woman to win back-to-back gold medals in the 100m Atlanta Olympics. In recognition of her phenomenal achievements she was awarded the annual Jesse Owens Award twice, which is presented to the top American athlete in track and field each year.

No words can describe the strength of Gail's character better than her own: "Whenever faced with a challenge, I dig deep within myself and summon my spiritual and physical forces. This gives me the focus, determination, perseverance and support I need to succeed... When I look at what I've accomplished during my life thus far, I realise I've been truly blessed. Now I want to share my good fortune by passing it on and helping others. Then, I'll consider myself a true champion."

Gail temporarily stopped competing in 2005 to give birth to her first child, but she returned again a year later. In February 2007, at the age of 40, she won the 60m hurdles event in 7.86 seconds which is just a fraction off the record she set in 2003. All I can say is WOW!... What a courageous and successful athlete and what an example of 100% pure positive energy! We can all learn from Gail's fantastic spirit as I have done.

Margaret Thatcher

Although my family was once very interested and active in politics and local government, since my early 20s I have not been politically inclined. However, during my childhood and teenage years, after witnessing situations which led me to believe that women were downtrodden and the weaker sex, along came Margaret Thatcher to run our country. FANTASTIC!

Although, like any human being she no doubt made mistakes, which a lot of politically minded people would dwell upon, the fact remains: she was a woman who launched herself into what was then a man's world. She earned herself the respect of the British public who voted her in to the highest political position possible as Prime Minister... more than once. I would often watch Margaret Thatcher on the television and admire her strength, power and confidence. Margaret Thatcher highlighted to me that irrespective of your gender... ANYTHING IS POSSIBLE!

Mother Teresa 1910 - 1997

Mother Teresa

Mother Teresa is, in my eyes, one of the most special human beings ever to have lived. She came to Ireland as an Albanian immigrant and after training in Dublin as a nun, was sent to Calcutta.

It was there that she came across a woman lying outside a hospital and comforted her until she died. She decided there and then to leave the convent and spend her life helping the poorest of the poor in India, earning her the name "Saint of the Gutters."

Although she had no funds, she started an open air school for children. With the assistance of voluntary helpers and financial support she then extended the scope of her work.

In 1950 she started her own order, "The Missionaries of Charity," whose primary task was to love and care for people that nobody was prepared to look after. This order now undertakes relief work in the aftermath of floods, epidemics and famine and helps refugees in Asia, Africa, and Latin America. It also has centres in North America, Europe and Australia where alcoholics, homeless people and AIDS sufferers are cared for. From an organisation that started with just 12 sisters in India, it now has over 3,000 sisters working in 517 missions across 100 countries.

For over 50 years, Mother Teresa devoted herself to helping the poor, providing them with the practical basics to live and more importantly, her love and respect. This deep compassion for others was recognised with the Nobel Peace Prize in 1979. Towards the end of her life, Mother Teresa suffered from heart problems and also caught malaria. Although she passed away in 1997 at the age of 87, her humanitarian work is still acclaimed throughout the world.

"Let us make one point, that we meet each other with a smile, when it is difficult to smile. Smile at each other, make time for each other in your family."

Mother Teresa

"God doesn't require us to succeed; he only requires that you try."

Mother Teresa

"We don't want much; we just want to change the world!"

Nik and Eva Speakman

"Nik and Eva Speakman, life coaches to the stars, could never be described as ordinary. They live in a castle with a fleet of super cars and speak only in positive psychobabble. But, as their series shows, there is a reason stars shell out their cash - the Speakmans' methods work."

The Times

Our mission...

Most people find the subject of changing human perspective quite complex. Our aim is to make the complex simple and thus help change the world... We firmly believe that it is our mission to make people's lives better and as professional life coaches we aim to help them become happier, kinder and more constructive individuals. As one national newspaper once said, we "transport people from mediocrity to the ultimate reaches of possibility."

Essentially, our mission is to change the world by changing the way people think about their lives and asking themselves why they were put on this planet. Big ideas? Unrealistic ambitions? Not really. Individuals make up a community. Communities make up society and societies make up countries. Countries make up the world! Whatever people think, that is our ultimate goal, whether we get there or not is not the issue. To us, the journey is just as important as the destination.

We help people rid themselves of the fears, phobias and habits that are ruining their lives. When people are freed from their inner limitations and actively set out to achieve their goals, their radiance and happiness shines a whole new, bright and wonderful light on everyone else and becomes infectious.

So many of the clients we treat feel that it is selfish to do something for themselves. If you feel this too, be assured this is a limiting belief stemming from conditioning that neither benefits you nor the people around you. Think of yourself as a happy and fulfilled pebble gliding confidently into a stream. As you gracefully enter the water, you cause a spectacular ripple effect that touches those around you with beauty, happiness, peace and harmony.

"Nik and I are navigators and map readers. We can guide people to their ultimate dreams and goals and help them to reach the most amazing destinations."

Eva Speakman

41

"We're great at what we do. We get amazing results. We know that this is what we're put on Earth to do. We change people's lives, there's no doubt about it."

Nik Speakman

Over the years, Eva and I have tackled a diverse range of problems including the fear of public speaking, lack of confidence, obsessive house cleaning, hair pulling, fear of vomiting, gambling, alcoholism, sex addiction and overeating. We tend to find that the most common issues seem to be confidence related. Usually, anyone who comes to us has reached what we called "threshold," the point where they are absolutely fed up and want to change their self destructive behaviour because it is completely ruining their lives.

They may have seen hypnotherapists, psychotherapists and sometimes even well known celebrity hypnotists, but nothing has worked. They have probably been visiting them for months, without success. In most cases, we have been able to undo decades of suffering (and the belief that they are incurable) and yet such is the effectiveness of our treatments, we are normally able to manage this in one or two sessions. We have the greatest of respect for anyone who decides that they want a career assisting others, however we just cannot understand why some practitioners need to sell consultations in blocks of ten or a dozen when changes can be achieved so quickly using our techniques.

When filming our TV series, we were often given only one afternoon to assess and treat the contributors. One of the most spectacular short sessions involved a lady who was petrified of ALL animals. At work, she was unable to walk to buy lunch in case she came in contact with a dog, or even a duck in the local park! She became hysterical when reliving a childhood experience involving a dog attack. Yet in less than four hours she was stroking our cat Chester and a week later she was considering buying a puppy. Positively life changing! How grateful we are to have the best job in the world!

Some people may be skeptical about what we do and say that it is just an American self-help fad and could attract the wrong kind of practitioners. We are completely aware of these criticisms and all we can say is that along with all our experience and diplomas, we've got a PhD in results! Our amazing success rate speaks for itself. Although we have many qualifications, we know that our clients would rather have results than see certificates hanging on our walls. All our therapies are based upon proven techniques and methods that we have learned through our years of study, training, personal experience and practice. We have then adapted them for maximum effect. When you are dealing with negative thought patterns that literally dominate someone's life, you have to create bigger, bolder, brighter and more dramatic memories and scramble the old and powerfully established ones. Everything we do and the techniques we follow have been tried and tested and they definitely work, as you will have seen if you watched our hit TV series A LIFE COACH LESS ORDINARY, which is now being shown in many different countries around the world.

Our aim is to discover the root of the problem and then, like a computer with a program that we don't want anymore, we scramble the program until it's as good as deleted. Our methods may look quite bizarre. Some make people cry, some make them laugh and some make them feel absolutely awful. In fact, Eva and I don't like a few of the things we have to do, but it's all about results. After all, our clients don't come to see us for sympathy; they come to us for help! Lots of people have told us that they consider us to be like the parents they wished they'd had because we genuinely care about their welfare and tell them what they *need* to hear, not just what they want to hear.

We are so proud of what we have achieved and love the work that we do. To see a happy confident person suddenly appear is hugely emotional. They walk out of our doors transformed. How fantastic is that? We just want to change people's perception of the world so that they too will realise that anything is possible and it is all there for the taking if you just remove "society's blinkers," open up your eyes' peripheral vision and reach out and take what you truly deserve. We want people to have the best possible experience of life they can and never to accept anything less than what they can be. All we want is to see and hear about people being successful. Success can be success in happiness, success in love, success in marriage or success in a hobby. In fact, it can be anything you want it to be.

Success is personal and wanting a better life is far, far from selfish. Quite the opposite, it means that you are prepared to assume responsibility, take control and change direction. No more blaming others, no more excuses, no more self sacrifice... The people you love, and who love you, will see all the good it's doing and follow your example. So you'll be multiplying the benefits by seeing the positive side effects all around you.

So join us for a magical journey into Speakman World, where everything is turbo-charged with positive energy and absolutely ANYTHING IS POSSIBLE. You don't believe in the tooth fairy. You don't believe in Santa Claus. You've got it all wrong, because the Speakmans are all of those things! **We give magic to people and make their dreams come true and we can make people hugely, HUGELY HAPPY!**

"Do it. Do it now!
The only thing that comes
to he who waits is old age."

Nik Speakman

2.

Dreams and goals

"You compromise your future if you live in the past."

Nik Speakman

your **fantasic life** starts here!

Reading this book will be the first step towards your new FANTASTIC LIFE! You may not be feeling that fantastic right now otherwise why would you be looking for help? In fact, you might be feeling pretty fed up with the way things are. You want to achieve happiness, fulfillment and success, but it's just not working for you.

The good news is that if you are willing to face up to the **truth about what is holding** you back and change the things that you are doing, we *guarantee* **that you will see great** results. When you make even the smallest changes, starting today, you will see massive changes several years down the line. It's like a space craft adjusting its direction by a couple of degrees; eventually it will end up light years away from its original destination!

We are going to show you how you can manage your own thinking, deal with situations that you have always found difficult and kick out those self-defeating habits once and for all. We are going to take you into the future so you can deal with issues that are preying on your mind and clouding your vision of the road ahead. We will give you new choices, new ways of thinking and open your eyes to a life that is bright with possibilities.

So sit back...and prepare for blast off...

10 - 9 - 8 - 7 - 6 - 5 - 4 - 3 - 2 - 1

We dare you to live the best life you can, NOW!

GOAL SETTING IS WISHFUL THINKING FOR REALISTS!

From a Canadian blue collar family trailer park family, with a sickly, hysterical mother and a manic depressive father, Jim Carrey worked 8-hour shifts after school, scrubbing toilets at the local Titan Wheels factory to help pay the bills. The experience hardened his will to escape to a better life. At 16, he dropped out of school because his grades were so poor. He concentrated instead on his solo comedy act and finally headed to Hollywood to be a stand up comedian. He struggled from job to job and was always broke. To help him focus (although he didn't know it at the time) he wrote a post dated cheque to himself for services rendered for the sum of 20 million dollars and kept it in his wallet. He subsequently and poignantly placed this cheque in his father's suit pocket at his funeral. The cheque was made payable in 1996, the same year he received exactly that amount for his portrayal of Chip Douglas in *The Cable Guy*. What an amazing dream! What an amazing goal! What an amazing vision!

Visionaries understand that the greatest actions in life begin with a dream. A dream is a "vision" of how you want things to be. If you dismiss dreams as fanciful ideas that will never happen, then that is exactly what they will be: fanciful ideas that will never happen. But when you believe it CAN be done and are willing to do what it takes to get there, your dream is just the starting point for reaching your goals.

> "All successful people men and women are big dreamers. They imagine what their future could be, ideal in every respect, and then they work every day toward their distant vision, that goal or purpose."
>
> Brian Tracy

> "Once you have a clear picture of your goals, you can organise your life around them."
>
> Nik Speakman

Occasionally people say to us, my life's great, there's nothing you can do to help me. But when we ask where they think they will be in ten years time they don't know the answer. The thing is, if you don't know where you are going, how will you appreciate and enjoy it when you get there? If you just stick to the same routine on autopilot, living from one day to the next, are you really going to experience the real fulfillment of life?

So many people are like back seat drivers of life. They watch the road and never relax. They feel tense and distrustful and are just waiting for the next potential accident to appear around the corner. They are not in control and are therefore unable to steer themselves to success. Life for them is an endless journey of fear and helplessness. They blame everyone else for their problems and take out their frustrations on their own family. (How sad it is for a child being transported along a rough and scary road by a parent who does not care about the state of their own life, never mind anyone else's.)

When you take control, you can change the route, go at your own pace, appreciate the scenery AND get to your chosen destination! What's more, your passengers will enjoy the ride and learn that clarity, direction and positivity gets you places.

Some years ago we read an interesting article about an assessment of students who were about to graduate from an American university in 1950. They were asked if they had any specific visions of their future and if they had documented these aspirations in the context of a goal. Of the all the graduates that year only 10% had any structured goals and only 3% had actually written them down. Some 20 years later, the students were contacted again. Unfortunately some had since died, yet all of the goal setters in the 3% group were healthy, alive and well plus they were more successful and financially better off than all of the remaining students put together!

Individuals who are most successful in life take the future into consideration with every decision they make in the present. We always say that tragedy doesn't lie in not reaching your goals; tragedy is when you have no goals to reach. The first and most vital thing you can do is to work out what it is you *really* want.

first
have a **target**

How could you play darts without a dart board? Archery without a target? Clay pigeon shooting without clays? Running a race with no finishing line? There would be darts, arrows, pellets and people here there and everywhere... There would be no winners, no organisation and it would end up a hazard to others who would find themselves in the firing line.

Is it any wonder that people without specific targets to aim for become frustrated with life and feel restless and unfulfilled? Vague generalities just don't work! So many people live their lives without aims or goals and this is so often the reason for their distress and frustration. We usually achieve what we set out to do. And even if we don't, we are always a lot closer than if we didn't have a target. The fact is, if you have a target, even if you miss, you will be a damn sight closer to living your dreams.

START...WRITE NOW!

Creating the content of your life is like going on a shopping trip. How many times have you been to the supermarket without a shopping list and forgotten half the things you wanted only to return with bags full of stuff you didn't really need? If you go to the supermarket with a shopping list, you'll come home with everything you need (or a close alternative) and a few treats besides. Goal setting is like writing your life's shopping list and is paramount to success. Goal setting is life changing and should never ever be underestimated.

It's sometimes hard to think what your heart really desires because we are so conditioned to put other people first and not to be selfish. Turn the page for a fantastic exercise that will help you express your true ambitions. The trick is to think of your shopping list as being something magical and FUN instead of purely practical and boring.

"Shoot for something specific. Even if you miss you'll be closer than if you just shoot aimlessly........and you'll cause less damage!"

Eva Speakman

> *"Everyone has the potential inside them to achieve great things, but our potential can just get trampled out on the treadmill of everyday life."*
>
> Eva Speakman

We literally got into the Christmas spirit to help British TV actor Scott Wright discover what he really wanted out of life.

★ Create a Christmas wish list ★

Imagine that you are a child looking forward to Christmas and writing a wish list for Santa. Children never consider the possibility of *not* being able to have something or who will buy their gift or the costs involved... You are in the land of your dreams, where absolutely anything is possible and your size, weight, academic capabilities, family, confidence levels are all irrelevant.

The key is to NOT think rationally. That way you will be less hesitant about saying what you want. A slight diversion of where you are, for example imagining you are on a magic carpet gliding over hills, dales and babbling brooks, or floating on a cloud will help your deeper subconscious desires to emerge more freely. When you feel that you are in this special place then begin writing down all the things that you want to achieve this week and over the next 20 years.

You may find that you can just write and write and easily list all the items you want in your life. If you are still having trouble identifying what it is you are aiming for, don't worry, over the page there are some prompts to spark your imagination.

My dreams...

How do I want to express myself?

What do I want to achieve?

What do I aspire to own?

How can I make a contribution to the world?

What would you like to learn?

Do you want to speak a foreign language?

Have you always wanted to play an instrument?

Did you ever want to paint, sing or dance?

Do you want to lose weight?

Have you wanted to get fit?

Have you wanted to run a marathon or raise money for a specific charity?

Do you feel you deserve a monthly pampering session at the beauty salon?

Did you want to take up, or continue playing tennis, running, badminton, swimming...

What are the character traits you'd like to develop?

Do you want to laugh more, be more understanding and more appreciative?

Do you want to be less judgmental, less angry and less envious?

Do you want to break patterns of frustration or rejection?

Do you want to contribute more and volunteer to help in a soup kitchen or animal sanctuary?

Do you want to conquer your fear of flying, your fear of heights, your fear of public speaking or spiders?

What kind of relationships do you want?

Do you want to meet someone special?

Do you want to build closer family bonds?

Would you like to visit an old friend or old flame?

Who do you want your friends to be?

Who do YOU want to be?

Where do you see yourself professionally and financially?

Do you want to be a supervisor, manager or director?

Do you have specific goals for your company?

Do you want your company to be more environmentally aware?

Do you want to design and patent something?

Do you want to be famous?

How much money would you need so you no longer have to work?

By what age do you want to achieve financial independence?

Do you want to work less and have more family time?

When do you want to retire?

What "toys" do you dream of owning?

Do you want to buy a holiday home, a new house, boat or even an island?

Do you want a private jet? Helicopter... Harley Davidson?

What do you want to experience?

Would you like to attend a film premier, a Broadway show or a major concert?

Do you want to spend Christmas in the Caribbean, go to Disney, travel across the United States in an RV or be one of the first tourists to travel on board the space shuttle?

Do you want to visit the pyramids of Egypt or swim with dolphins?

There are no limits!

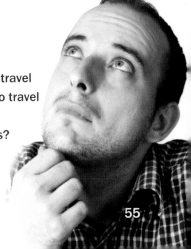

"When our memories outweigh our dreams we have grown old."

Bill Clinton

"Dreams are renewable. No matter what our age or condition there are still untapped possibilities within us and new beauties waiting to be born."

Dale Turner

Where will you be 10 years from now?

Here's an exercise you may find quite challenging but fun! First of all, you will need a pen and some writing paper and at least half an hour of quiet time on your own. This exercise involves going into the future and imagining yourself 10 years from now. (To get an idea of how much you can achieve, just think for a minute what your life was like 10 years ago and how different it is today.)

Now picture yourself another 10 years older. Has your career progressed? Have you changed jobs, gained new qualifications or did you start a new business? Think about the aging process and what it has meant to you. Have you gained weight, recovered from an illness, lost weight and become fitter, been through a divorce or met someone new, or even all of the above!

Imagine that the intervening years have passed and you are writing to a trusted friend. So start the letter "Dear… (friend's name)" and date the letter as if it was being written 10 years from now. Tell your friend what a great life you have now. Describe your home, your close relationships, the car you drive, the clothes you wear and what you look like. Say what you have done to make the world a better place. Go into as much detail as you can. Describe how successful you are and how you achieved your goals. Tell them how you overcame any problems that you had 10 years ago (i.e. now). Once again, go into as much detail as you can.

Explain how you are spending your time and your beliefs and your thoughts about the past and future. Do not worry about the "reality" of your ideas. Just express your thoughts as they emerge. You are visualising your ideal future. You can amuse and delight yourself by making your visions as colourful and exciting as you wish. If you find yourself laughing as you write this letter you are on the right track!

My own letter from my future…

This is a fantastic exercise that I did just for a bit of fun well before I knew the true power that it holds. I wrote my letter whilst I was still living with my parents and I addressed it to a friend in Poland. I had imagined that I was now aged 30 and I described my life. I then filed it away and totally forgot about it. I found it again about 15 years later and couldn't believe the accuracy; so many things had come true. My favourite quotes were that I said I lived in a great big old mansion house with big black electric gates with a crest on them and I was married and my husband was called Nick. Awesome!

57

The Speakman dream to reality success formula

Because goals are so vital to happiness and success you must **WRITE THEM DOWN**. Just think what would happen if you didn't keep a record of special dates and meetings; you would miss them. Your goals are important appointments that you need to keep! Here's our highly effective 10-step guide to putting your dream plans into action.

1. Put yourself into the right frame of mind to envisage your dreams following the Christmas list steps on page 52.

2. Grab a piece of paper and divide it into two columns. In the first column, list 50 things (it can be more but not less!) things you want to do, own, learn, achieve, visit or change. Include everything that you ever dreamed would happen to you in your lifetime.

3. In the second column set yourself a time limit and specify what it is next to each of your fabulous dreams. For example, "within 1 year," "within 3 years," "5 years," "10 years," "15 years" and "20 years."

4. On another piece of paper create a separate list for all of your "within 1 year" goals, leaving a few lines between each one.

5. Underneath each goal, describe how you will feel if you do not achieve it and how it will negatively impact your life.

6. Now state how you will feel when you achieve this goal. To really do this effectively close your eyes and visualise yourself when you have reached this goal. Experience how wonderful and fulfilling it feels. See, hear, feel and smell that tremendous sense of achievement. You can create motivation by visualising the rewards of your effort clearly. (A good salesman will have you living in your imaginary dream home in minutes). Learn to be your own salesman and MAKE IT REAL.

7. To increase your confidence and motivation, think about the things that you have already achieved in your life that you once thought were really challenging, frightening or couldn't do. It could be getting married, having children, passing an exam, passing your driving test, winning an award, speaking in public, getting the job you wanted, doing something for charity or running a marathon! Choose five of your best achievements and write them down... NOW YOU KNOW ANYTHING IS POSSIBLE AS YOU HAVE ACHIEVED HUGE GOALS ALREADY.

8. Imagine you are at the bottom of a ladder. Your goal is at the top. All you need to do is take one small step up. Forget about the number of rungs or the ladder's height. Just think about placing your foot on the first rung. The more rungs you climb, the more your confidence will grow. You will get momentum, you will be capable of taking on bigger challenges and you will soon reach the top of the ladder.

9. Consider what would that first step would be... a phone call, looking something up on the Internet, or going to the library. Something as small and as simple as that.

10. Take that first step RIGHT NOW! We meet so many people who tell us they have huge ambitions for the future, but it's all, "One day I am going to do this and one day I am going to do that." Forget "I'll start Monday" or "When I'm home from my holiday..." or "In the New Year, I'll..." **Just DO IT NOW!!!**

The great news is you wake to a new day every day and a new minute is starting RIGHT NOW. So celebrate each new minute, each new hour and each new day and welcome it with passion, energy, focus and drive!

MAKE THAT MINUTE, HOUR OR DAY *START NOW* !!!!

More ways to bring your goals closer to you

1. Buy yourself a stylish folder or file and start filling it with images of your dreams. Put in things that will be a part of your future life (use magazines or go online to find images and start collecting relevant objects). It may include cars, your ideal house... Add a photo of you and your loved ones looking happy! You are creating a collage or a scrap book of your future. Keep looking at it regularly to remind yourself where you are heading.

2. Write yourself two cheques for the amount of money you will earn and stick one in your book. Then place the other in a prominent position in your home. Write an agreement like a legal and binding document of all the things that you promise to do for yourself. For example, you might specify going to the gym, quitting smoking, being more positive or looking for the good in people... When you are happy with all the details sign it.

3. Talk about your plans to others. This makes you accountable and helps to fix your goals even more firmly in your mind and makes them an important part of your reality.

Updating your goal list

When you have created your list of "Within 1 Year" goals, look at it every day. Put a monthly note in your diary to remind yourself to read through your full goal list and to remind yourself what you are aiming for and stay focused. Twice a year (January 1st and June 1st are great days) take a step back and re-evaluate the list and create a new one. Take off any goals that no longer inspire you and add new ones. As the years go by, you will have done one of three things:

1. Achieved your goal
2. Decided it is not what you want after all
3. By seeing your goal again it will add more momentum to make you feel even more positive towards it and you'll want to achieve it even more

And so the magic fairy dust has been sprinkled...
Enjoy your success you remarkable, fantastic
and AWESOME ACHIEVER!!!

"Your future can be anything you desire once you have taken the first step of deciding what it is you want."

Nik Speakman

How has goal setting worked for us?

The great thing about creating a goal list is that it is not written in stone. It can change as both the years and your personality progress. But what does happen when you start to make your aspirations visible by writing them down and remembering to read them regularly is that suddenly your dreams become a reality.

From the moment Eva and I embarked on what we thought was the time consuming and pointless task of documenting everything that we hoped would happen to us, it was like magic fairy dust being sprinkled on our life. All of a sudden, things started to happen!

Just a few of the dreams that have come true for Eva include getting married and having two children (a girl and a boy), owning a beautiful home, visiting her grandfather in Australia, running the London Marathon (she has applied three times and not got in, but three rejections warrant a guaranteed place next time!) being a life coach, meeting Arnold Schwarzenegger, going to Hawaii and writing a book.

Some of my dreams that are now a fantastic reality are being married to the woman of my dreams with whom I have two fantastic, healthy children, having the knowledge and ability to assist people change their lives for the better, owning the exotic cars I always wanted, being fit and healthy, having a toned muscular body, having a glorious home, being able to work because I want to and not because I have to and most of all knowing that through the media and television that we have helped to positively influence many people who we haven't even met. Oh, and of course, not only having the best job in the world, but also the best working partner too!

61

Look how these achievers have Speakmanned their lives!

Beki

I heard about Nik and Eva when I was at a low point in my career. I'd just quit a job that I wasn't happy in with no real idea of what I wanted long term. I was finding it difficult to know what direction to head in. After just two sessions with the Speakmans, I felt rejeuvenated. They managed to unearth hopes and dreams that had been buried within me for years and showed me practical ways to move towards realising them, rather than just spending my life vaguely wishing for them.

Just over a year later and I've got a great job with excellent prospects. I've bought my first house, I am single for the first time in nine years, I am writing a book and I'm loving it all! While it's not been a smooth ride, the downs have been made easier knowing that the ups won't be far behind and that I'm in control all the way.

Donna

The Speakmans have changed my life in many subtle ways. I have endured a challenging few years of late. First, my brother was in a coma due to a brain injury following a car accident. Then I had a pelvis operation which went wrong and left me unable to walk without sticks for two years. But by adopting a naturally "glass half full" attitude to life and using a few stolen techniques I skimmed from watching the Speakmans on TV, I am feeling on top of the world and ready to go.

Watching Eva exuberantly bouncing on her mini trampoline made me buy one too and now my hip is almost as good as new. Today I only have a slight limp very infrequently much to the amazement of many of my friends and family. Just a little technique or lifestyle change snatched here and there can make all the difference.

> "We are dream catchers.
> We encourage people to
> take any and every action
> possible to become the
> best that they can be!"
>
> Nik Speakman

Paul

I am 38 and married with a 6-year old son. I have worked in car sales for about 15 years as a sales trainer teaching groups of salespeople how to sell cars and finance facilities. My problems are that I have a massive addiction to pain killers, I also smoke cigarettes and my relationship with my wife (my best friend) is difficult. I know there are many people with bigger issues than me so I do not feel sorry for myself.

The good news is that one day I sat down to watch a TV program called A LIFE COACH LESS ORDINARY and was completely fascinated by it. The Speakmans are obviously very good at what they do. But something that really shone through for me was their absolute sincerity towards themselves, their family and to other people. Sincerity. What a great word! It is now a goal of mine to show more of it.

The Speakmans have inspired me to make some serious changes to my attitude and to start taking control. Things are starting to move forward already and life is steadily improving. (I would say it's FANTASTIC but I will save that word until I achieve everything I've set out to do.) When you have been down in the dumps and generally negative for a while, if you start to write down a few goals you suddenly think, "Where have I been all these years?" It's like suddenly realising you do have a life not just an existence.

"To **fail** means you have gone down a route that did not end where you had hoped. But you have still **travelled** and you will be **wiser** and **stronger** for your journey... **and better equipped** to set out again in a direction that will take you **even faster** to your destination."

THE FAILURE MYTH

Everyone makes mistakes. Everyone will fail at something. Well, we have we got news for you! In Speakman World there is no such thing as failure and no such thing as mistakes. When you attempt to do something you will always get a result. It might not be the result that you want, but it's still a result; it's not a failure. Think about it. If Nick Faldo hit a few balls off course, would he have walked off the green never to play again? Would Arnold Schwarzenegger have got on the next plane home to Austria after the first bad audition? Would J.K. Rowling have thrown her book in the fire after the first rejection? Would Thomas Edison have given up after his thousandth attempt to invent the lightbulb? Of course not. They would adjust their game, try new tactics and learn from what wasn't successful. Trying and failing is an integral part of success.

You may have always been afraid of taking the plunge (maybe you were the child who sat shivering at the side of the swimming pool). But why should you stay in a job you hate instead of doing something you enjoy? Why should you stay in a soulless marriage instead of being with someone who makes you feel valued? If you hate being overweight, stop the suffering NOW. Why should you carry on hating yourself for not having the guts to change the situation? If you are constantly worried about failing you are condemning yourself to a future of inertia and dissatisfaction.

Constantly beating yourself up about things that have gone wrong is another thing that people are good at. We meet so many intelligent, kind and talented individuals who walk round obsessing about some opportunity they missed or something they did that ended disappointingly. Failing does not make you a loser. Yet some people will still stick this invisible label on their forehead and wonder why everything keeps going wrong for them. What happens is that everyone starts to treat them like a loser... and then the cycle is complete.

In Speakman World we do not believe in labels either. Inside every single one of us there is a person with unique depth and talent. It's time to start believing in your abilities. When you want something, think of the outcome, then just go for it. If you don't get what you want first time, instead of asking yourself what you haven't achieved ask yourself what you *have* achieved. What have you learnt? How can you do better next time? If what you are doing isn't working TRY A DIFFERENT APPROACH... GO IN A NEW DIRECTION. KEEP TAKING ACTION, UNTIL YOU GET THE RESULTS YOU WANT!!!

Finally, remember that the definition of perfectionism is continuing to work on something well past the point where your effort is adding meaningful value. Perfectionism steals your time and energy. **You don't have to get it right, you just have to get it going!**

"J think J'd like to be remembered as someone who beat the odds through just plain determination… that J persevered. Because J think that being somewhat of a pest to life, constantly plaguing and pursuing, will bring results."

Sylvester Stallone

"People never fail! They just give up trying."

Nik and Eva Speakman

Inspiring lives..

On July 6th 1946 Jackie Stallone gave birth to her first son Sylvester in the charity ward of a hospital in Hell's Kitchen, New York. At a whopping 13lb, he was yanked, forced and eventually pulled into the world with the use of forceps. This drastic procedure severed a nerve above his jaw, leaving parts of his mouth and chin paralysed. As a result, his eyelid and his lip drooped and suffered a speech impediment that would take years of therapy to overcome.

Sylvester was an intelligent guy, but was often wrongly assumed to have learning difficulties because of his slurred diction. His facial disfigurement also led to him being nicknamed Mr Potato Head (and worse!) at school. Too scared to answer back because of his speech, he clammed up and became surly and difficult. He coped by becoming a risk taker and by thinking up fantasies in which he was the brave hero and champion of the underdog.

As a straight F student, Sylvester's childhood was an endless run of people pushing him, punching him and telling him he was ugly, useless and thick. At home, his father was also very critical of him. If he did dare to answer back, his father would beat him. (Apparently he would whistle before hitting him, and when Sylvester became a big star, the still traumatised actor banned whistling from his sets, due to the neuroassociations he had developed.)

After studying drama at the University of Miami, life was still tough as Sylvester struggled to find work. In 1969 he headed back to New York City to pursue his passion for screenwriting. He read many books on the subject and wrote endlessly. Continuing with his acting ambitions, he also went to numerous open auditions. But the answer was always the same: he was just another average mumbling Marlon Brando wannabe with muscles.

By now Sylvester was married, but pride prevented him from asking for financial support from his family. He lived in a rundown apartment with his wife, who constantly pecked at him to go out and get a "real job." Sylvester knew he was a talented writer and actor and refused to accept anything less than he was capable of and deserved. After hitting financial rock bottom, his wife left him. He then lost his home and resided in hostels and tatty accommodation with his faithful dog for company. While he was sitting in a bar reflecting on his predicament, Sylvester watched the great Muhammed Ali in a boxing match on the TV. Afterwards he sat down and wrote continuously without even stopping to sleep. With dedication, energy, enthusiasm and belief, he created the screenplay for what would become his massive hit film *Rocky*!

At this point, the struggling would-be playwright and actor was so destitute that he had to sell his beloved dog outside a convenience store. He got just enough money for a meal and one night's accommodation. Still he continued to wander from one movie producer to the next trying to sell his idea for a film about a young boxer trying to make a name for himself in the 1940s. Regrettably, not many people took him seriously. Those that did promptly withdrew their offers when Sylvester told them that the proviso to him selling his script was that he starred as the main character. Although he only had about $100 to his name, Sylvester did not give in. He did not accept second best and refused to compromise his goal.

He sat in movie makers' receptions during the day and slept outside movie makers' offices all night. Eventually a production company offered him a reasonable sum of money for the screenplay. But because of the stipulation that Sylvester should take the lead role, it was agreed that he would only be paid a share of the profits in case the film flopped.

The rest as they say is history... Only to add that Sylvester later returned to the convenience store and waited outside for many days until he spotted the man that had bought his dog. It is reported that he had to buy the dog back for more than ten times the amount for which he had sold it! So what is the moral of this story? Well yes, of course the usual don't settle for second best, and if you don't succeed then try, and try again. But more importantly, it illustrates one of our favourite sayings:

PERSISTENCE WILL EVENTUALLY OUTSHADOW ANYTHING, EVEN TALENT!

role models are the test vehicles for your life

What do all the successful people Eva and I have mentioned have in common? They have all been strongly influenced by someone who impressed them a great deal. John F. Kennedy was Bill Clinton's role model, Eleanor Roosevelt was Hillary Clinton's and Thomas Edison was the inspirational character that drove Henry Ford (who even hung his picture near his work area).

Modelling yourself on a successful person is a brilliant short cut to being the person you want to be. Instead of spending years trying to work out what works, you just look at the role model who best personifies what you want to achieve. Study them, find out as much as you can about the way they think, read their biography, emulate their style, their self-discipline and their approach to life. All you have to do is copy what they are doing. If you copy it exactly, you will get the same results. If you put enough hours in and approach something with enough clarity then you will get there every time.

As well as emulating someone from a distance, look for people around you, who have character traits that you want and follow their formula. If you want to lose weight and get healthy, make friends with people who eat healthily and work out. If you want to be a kinder, happier person introduce yourself to some kind, happy people. If you want to be more successful in business, socialise with successful business people and company directors. Just one word of warning, choose your role models carefully!

Who has influenced who?

"When I was starting out … I thought Debbie Harry was the coolest chick in the universe." - Madonna

"Madonna is my role model she's such a powerful woman. I love Gwenyth Paltrow, she's an actress I aspire to be like…" - Kirsten Dunst

"Jeane Kirkpatrick [a human rights advocate] was a role model for me as an academic and policymaker…" - Secretary Condoleezza Rice

"Sally Ride [one of my role models] made it possible for anyone to become an astronaut." - Ellen Ochoa, the first Hispanic woman to be accepted into the NASA space shuttle program.

"Maya Angelou was a role model for me. Growing up, reading her book, 'I Know Why the Caged Birds Sing' really kind of opened up my life in a way that made me think for the first time that being colored and being poor had some validation." - Oprah

The Behaviour Igniter Exercise

1. Close your eyes and think of the person you wish to emulate.
2. Replay your memory of that person, noticing in particular their posture, their tone of voice and their mannerisms. What would they say and how they would behave?
3. Like a movie director make any changes to make them completely perfect for you.
4. Now float over to them and into their body.
5. See the world through their eyes. Imagine what they hear and what they see. Feel their confidence.
6. Do an ecology check. Does this new behaviour fit in with your values and beliefs?
7. If anything is not as it should be or changes need to be made, float back out of their body and go back to being the movie director and make any changes required.
8. Now see yourself stepping in to their body. So you can see the world through their eyes, with their strength and qualities that you admire!
9. If you need to have this person's qualities for a specific event, think of the future event, and see yourself using this new behaviour. Imagine yourself performing in the situation.
10. Repeat several times until you get a real sense that you are actually walking in their shoes... not just following in their footsteps.

How this exercise has worked for us

Our first session on live TV in 2004 was quite nerve racking. No time delays, no rehearsals and only 8 minutes to get our message across! The more we thought about it, the more pressure we put ourselves under. The voice in our heads said things like, "What if you just freeze?... What if we don't speak with clarity and our message could be misconstrued?" So we used this fantastic tool, The Behaviour Igniter Exercise and based our model on one of our favourite, confident and amusing TV presenters, Jay Leno!

Inspiring lives...

© Richard Y

Can you imagine the world without Harry Potter? That could have easily happened if Jo Rowling had not pursued her dream. Eva and I often wonder what great stories that nearly reached the world, yet the author gave up just when they were at the closest to getting their work published.

Joanne K. Rowling once had limited time, very limited money and limited self belief. But her drive to share her world of fantasy and magic surpassed the obstacles in her way. As a single mother, with her baby asleep in a pushchair and a cup of cold coffee by her side, she wrote the first of the astronomically successful *Harry Potter* series of books sitting at the back of Nicholson's café in Edinburgh. One of

the owners remembers his regular customer saying, "She would just rock the pram back and forward with one hand and write away with the other."

Her struggles certainly did not end when the manuscript had been completed. Aged of 28 and recently divorced, Jo was living on state benefits in a flat infested with mice and often worried that she would have enough money to last the week. She wrote *Harry Potter* to pay off her gas bills, but her first attempts to persuade a publishing company to accept her book all met with rejection. With her self esteem at rock bottom, she realised that her dreams would not pay the bills so she took another teaching job, which was a job she had done earlier in her life.

In fact, Jo's career path had taken several directions. After graduating from Exeter University where she studied French, (she had wanted to go to Oxford but was turned down), She obtained her degree in 1986 and over the next few years held a variety of secretarial jobs, including one at a publishing firm, where ironically, she had to send out rejection letters to hopeful authors! Jo soon accepted that she was not cut out for administrative work describing herself as "the worst secretary ever, very disorganised." She found her mind wandering off during meetings and would be writing story ideas instead of taking notes!

Jo also worked as a bilingual secretary for Amnesty International. It was during a four-hour delayed train journey on her way up to Manchester that she first had the idea for a story about a boy called Harry Potter who attended a school of wizardry. From the beginning, she planned a seven-volume series, saying, "I decided that it would take seven years, from the ages of 11 to 17, inclusive, to train as a wizard..."

Sadly, it was around this time when Jo was 26, that her mother lost her 10-year-long battle with multiple sclerosis at the age of 45. She never knew about her daughter's wonderful story ideas and this is something that has troubled Joanne ever since. "Barely a day goes by when I do not think of her," she said later. "There would be so much to tell her, impossibly much." Hoping to find a way to deal with her grief, Jo took a job in Portugal teaching English. Working in the afternoons and evenings left her free to concentrate on her writing in the morning.

In 1992, she married a journalist and they had a daughter, Jessica, who was named after Jo's heroine, Jessica Mitford. But just a year later, after a fight in which her husband threw her out of the house, Jo sought a divorce. She returned to live in Edinburgh near her sister, bringing her 3-month old daughter and a "half a suitcase full of papers covered with stories about Harry Potter."

Her intention was to start teaching again, but because it was a full-time job and she had a baby to care for single-handedly, there would have been no time to write. So she wrote obsessively nearly every evening and whenever her child was asleep during the daytime. The pressure was so intense that she said, "Sometimes I actually hated the book, even while I loved it."

With no job and little income, Jo asked for a grant from the Scottish Arts Council. She used the money to buy a computer. When her first novel was finally completed, she sent off the manuscript and waited to hear from the publishers and literary agents. However,

"I value courage beyond almost anything."

J.K. Rowling

> "It is our choices... that show what we truly are, far more than our abilities."
>
> J.K. Rowling

her morale took a battering as one by one they advised her that Harry Potter would not be successful. They thought it was too long, too slow and too literary for a children's story.

Jo found herself in the classic single-mother trap: unable to afford childcare so she could not go to work. For almost a year, until she got another teaching job, Jo and her daughter lived on £70 a week. She has since described her marital break up, financial hardship, loneliness and subsequent depression as the most turbulent part of her life.

After being rejected by nine publishers, eventually, in 1997, she sold her first novel to Bloomsbury for a modest £2,000. Even then, the publishing representative told her she would not make any money selling children's books. However, with the sale of the American rights for a record-breaking $100,000 advance for a children's book, Jo had enough money to give up teaching and write full time. It was a turning point that she pronounced to be the happiest moment of her life. The phone call with the offer came through just after midnight. Jo went to bed but couldn't sleep, describing her feelings as being "obviously delighted, but most of me was just frozen in terror."

Receiving the money though, was not as important to her as knowing that it had been confirmed that there was one thing she was good at. It was the realisation of her life's ambition: to be a published author after so many years of effort. (It had taken about six years for her to get her first book ready for printing.) Finally, she said, she "didn't feel like a waste of space anymore." Since then, her books have been best sellers all over the world. Jo's wealth has reached epic, almost legendary, proportions at over a £545 million and it's set to rise even further still! Indeed, the scale of her income is so great that it is hard to comprehend.

In 2001 she remarried in a private ceremony at her home in Scotland and later gave birth to a boy in 2003 and a girl in 2005. But despite her massive income, Jo and her family enjoy a normal, quiet family life. Her husband continues to work as a doctor in Edinburgh and her children all attend local state schools. Jo is reported to have said that she really does not like spending money

"J.K. Rowling is a role model to me because she writes excellent books, and the books are always great, which inspires me to write more."

Daniel in La Crescenta, California

and feels caught out and overwhelmed by her fame and fortune.

In fact, she has been steadily giving away huge chunks of her earnings to charity. She founded the Children's High Level Group to promote children's rights, particularly those of disabled children in care homes in Eastern Europe. She is world ambassador for the National Council for One-Parent Families and patron of the Multiple Sclerosis Society of Scotland. In addition, she has funded the making of a short film about domestic abuse and asked the official sponsor of her movies, Coca Cola, to donate $18m to charity. In 2001, the British government awarded her with an OBE.

Jo is also a patron of Maggie's Centres for cancer sufferers and after hearing about the plight of a nine-year-old cancer patient named Catie Hoch, Jo called her from her Edinburgh home when she heard that she only had weeks to live. Catie, who was an avid Harry Potter fan, listened intently as Jo read an unpublished story to her over the phone so that the little girl would know what happened before she passed away.

In February 2007, Jo announced that she had finished the seventh and final book in the *Harry Potter* series and said that she was "simultaneously heartbroken and euphoric" at saying goodbye to the magical world that had occupied her life for 17 years. During this incredible period, more than 325 million copies of the first six books have been sold worldwide.

Of her breathtaking success, Jo says, "I am an extraordinarily lucky person, doing what I love best in the world. I'm sure that I will always be a writer. It was wonderful enough just to be published. The greatest reward is the enthusiasm of the readers."

"Anything's possible if you've got enough nerve."

J.K. Rowling

73

3.

Finding time

IF TIME IS YOUR ENEMY, MAKE ORGANISATION YOUR WEAPON OF CHOICE!

So your goal is to buy a house in Spain? Spend more time with the kids? Lose your flabby stomach? Be fluent in Chinese...? The distance that stands between you and your dreams depends upon your quotas of two basic factors: TIME and PASSION. We'll talk about passion in the next chapter. If you have no time and are feeling constantly under pressure, reaching your goals will seem like an impossible task. You may even end up dumping them on the pile with all the other things on your endless "to do" list. So start by getting your house in order. Literally.

If you believe that untidiness and chaos make you look busy, or that being organised is for boring people you are kidding yourself. When everything around you is a mess, your life's a mess. You can't think straight, you can't find things, jobs take longer to do, important things get lost... and the look of it all is just disheartening! When you de-clutter your personal environment: your house, your car and your office, you are detoxing your mind and often getting a great physical workout at the same time! Whether it's Feng Shui or just basic cleaning, straightening out your environment puts you back in control and is a vital first step to making bigger changes in your life.

Organising because you "have to" or because you think your partner prefers things to be tidy is not the right approach (you'll feel like a slave!). Say to yourself that "you choose to de-clutter" instead of "you have to clean." You must keep in mind your goal. That must be your motivating force. It must come from inside YOU. Life is far easier and more comfortable when you have control of it. One of the best ways to help you focus on what is really important in your life is to clear out all the items in your home that are no longer use or value.

Clothes, books, paperwork and memorabilia tend to mount up and turn into obstacles and distractions that can throw your life off balance. How many times have you searched through racks of unworn, outdated shirts to find the one that fits and looks good? Trying to find an essential document among a pile of receipts and bills can create frustration that can lead forever to an association of paperwork with headaches. Don't let the chaos beat you! Take control of your space and ensure everything in it has its place. What's more, make sure it has earned that place on merit. Identify what is useful and/or valued and what is not.

Home Detox Program

1. Label some heavy duty bin liners: Trash, Donate, Sell, Keep.

2. Go through your cupboards, wardrobes and bookcases. Look at each item. Is it useful, worn out, do you like it, does it have bad memories? Only keep things you use, appreciate or make you happy.

3. Make a home inventory. Create a computer file for all your valuables (e.g. TV, jewellery, cars, computer.) Enter the item's value and any serial/model numbers and add a photo. When buying new items, update your inventory. This is also a useful resource for insurance purposes or if you decide to sell the goods on the Internet in the future.

4. Everything you keep should have a designated home. Invest in storage containers, boxes, bins, files, cases, baskets etc. and label them. Include a "may come in handy" container and when it is full get rid of something before you put anything else in!

5. Fix it or ditch it! Schedule a date to repair anything that is broken. If it has still not been done by then, get rid of it while it's on your mind.

6. Take photos of possessions you no longer need but don't want to forget, then dump your excess baggage or give it away.

7. Remember to clear out your makeup bag and travel bags. Old cosmetics (especially mascara), dirty disposable toothbrushes and stale toiletries are unhygienic and 100% pure clutter.

8. Teach your family to tidy as they go, especially the kids!

9. Organise your desktop and we mean your computer's too! Make sure anything that you have on your computer is correctly named and filed. It can be just as frustrating looking for lost items on a PC as it is in a cupboard! Delete out-dated material and transfer large files and photo collections into a plug-in vault. When you free up space in your computer it will run faster...and so will your mind!

10. Finally, give yourself a pat on the back! Have a luxurious treat; get your nails done, go for a massage, or dance naked in your clean and tidy kitchen!!!

> "If you want to live your best life and avoid dying with your dreams unrealised, you need to be organised."
>
> Eva Speakman

77

How we put the theory into action

Some years ago, a very close family member was feeling, as she put it, "depressed." She often said, "I'm a mess, my car is a mess, my life is a mess!" Being a family member we knew firsthand that her statement also extended to the state of her home.

The following weekend, we arrived on her doorstep with a bucket, rubber gloves, cloths, lots of rubbish bags and some good music! We cleared every room, cupboard, ornament, shelf and drawer. Days later the house was free from clutter and was sparkling. Instantly our relative said she felt as if a huge burden had been lifted. She said that somehow each day had brightened in an instant and this gave her the motivation to have a personal de-clutter too. Within three months she had a new look, a new wardrobe and a new job!

This transformation taught us something too. Since that day, the Home Detox Program is something that happens on a regular basis in the Speakman household. The great news is that after you practice something long enough it becomes a naturally conditioned way of life. So the clutter stops accumulating... things are put away after they are used and everyone just cleans as they go. When you have a busy life it is vital to keep your house in order, or you will soon get overwhelmed by the jobs that need doing and the pressure will become too much.

A home should be a sanctuary where you can unwind, relax and look at your surroundings and feel peaceful. Never underestimate the importance of a clean and lovely home. You will feel better, your family will feel better and guests will feel appreciated and welcomed.

Of course, we know that everyone has limited time and housework is often the first thing to suffer when your schedule is full. So make it easy on yourself and automate, delegate or delete the jobs that drain your time. We've added a few tips and ideas of our own on the next page to help you get started.

"When your house is a mess, your life's a mess!"

Nik and Eva Speakman

Dealing with the time drainers

The ultimate aim of de-cluttering is to free up as much time as you can to do the things you really love. As well as offloading material junk, think about the things that take up space in your day. Look at the way you approach everything you do. Is there a faster, more efficient alternative? Can you ask someone else to do it? Can the tasks be simplified? Here are a few suggestions that you may consider making into lifelong habits.

Going to the supermarket **Shop online**

Doing the housework **Employ a cleaner/do four two minute cleaning jobs in the morning and four in the evening. Have guests remove shoes when entering the house. Always put things away immediately, don't leave it until later. Also, teach the rest of the family to do so too!**

Cooking **Make double the amount and freeze it whenever you can.**

Getting ready for work/ **Prepare as much as you can in advance; make packed lunches and plan which clothes are to be worn the night before.**

Going to the bank **Pay bills by direct debit and use online banking**

Washing the car **Use a car wash or call a mobile valeting company.**

Ironing **Hang or fold clothes up as soon as they come out of the dryer or better still, off the washing line. Buy easy care clothes.**

Social occasions you don't enjoy **Say no!**

Long phone calls **Short emails.**

Long commutes to work **Work from home a few days a week or consider moving house. If this is not possible, invest in reading material that will expand and improve your mind. (If that's what you're doing right now, WELL DONE)**

Watching TV Turn it off!

...automate, delegate or delete!!!

79

Rebalancing your priorities

We all have a basic pattern of activities that we spend time on every day: work, family, exercise, hobbies, socialising. If one of these activities takes up too much of your time and energy it can have a negative knock-on effect. By pushing yourself too hard in one direction you can start to suffer symptoms of burn out. Alternatively, and even worse, you may feel overwhelmed, bad tempered, start making mistakes and use alcohol or other drugs to blur reality and bring down stress levels. It's important to be honest about your life balance and make adjustments for your sake and for the sake of people who are closest to you.

Separation, whether it is physical or mental, is the cause of many relationship breakdowns. If you are unable or unwilling to share your time more equally, you might regret the consequences. Don't overlook your partner, or the love, attraction and passion that initially brought you together. Have a "date" one evening or lunch-time each month. On your date, talk about when you first met and what you thought of each other. Remember your first impressions of each other, the first time you kissed and the first time you made love! If you are married, share your memories of the great things about your wedding day, places you have visited, events and parties you have attended or any other tremendous and fun things you have done together.

"To keep them alive and growing strongly, relationships need to be regularly cultivated, like a beautiful garden. If you don't turn the soil, you won't bring the nutrients to the surface!"

Eva Speakman

★ Your personal wheel of life

Label the wedges of the wheel with words that most apply to the areas in your life (those shown here are only an example). Now rate your satisfaction level from 0 – 10. When you join the marks, they *should* form a perfect circle!

If that's you then congratulations; your life is perfect! Seriously, we wouldn't expect your wheel to be anything near perfect. This exercise highlights the areas that you need to focus upon more, so you get the most out of life without making sacrifices to do so.

Even if you think that things are fine, having an uneven balance is like having a wonky wheel on a car; things won't run smoothly. Try this exercise just to see how much better it is when everything and everyone, *including your-self*, receives a fair share of your time and attention.

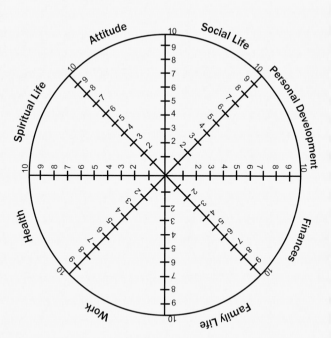

How did this work for us?

We refer to our Wheel of Life regularly to make sure we constantly maintain a balance across our life. This is so important as it is easy to get caught up in the humdrum aspects of everyday living if you don't.

The first time I plotted out my wheel of life it looked like more like a teapot! Completing the wheel highlighted to me that I was neglecting social time with my family and other things that mattered because I was wasting far too much time on superficial tasks. The whole exercise was so rewarding that I couldn't wait to try it on Eva. Curiously, Eva's wheel ended up looking like a teacup! That's probably why even before our wheels were circular we got on so well... we were made for each other!

81

FAILING TO PLAN IS PLANNING TO FAIL!

Here are some tips that we have learned to apply to our lives to avoid "hectic schedule syndrome" or inertia which are not conducive to reaching your goals:

1. Write things down. Don't rely on your memory!
2. Carry a notebook or digital recorder. You never know when you are going to have a great idea!
3. Say "no" to low priority requests, so you free up your time to spend on more important tasks.
4. Before committing to something stop and think before you say "Yes."
5. Reassess your activities. Sometimes it is better to stop doing an activity so you can spend your time doing something more valuable.
6. Busy is not always best. Ask yourself if what you are doing is accomplishing anything significant that will take you closer to your desired goal. Become outcome driven!
7. Remember, the two main time wasters are watching television and talking on the phone. If you need to create time, use emails and keep phone call time limited.
8. Continuously improve yourself! For example, attend a training program, or read a book.
9. Improving your knowledge is the most reliable path to success in life.
10. DO IT NOW. Do not procrastinate/contemplate or worry. Analysis = Paralysis!
    If some time is not regularly spent on achieving long range goals you can get stuck in a perpetual holding pattern of short term plans. This is where The Speakman Success Seven can add structure to your visions.

The Speakman Success Seven

Set aside one hour every day (we do this every evening) and write a list of seven things you need to do or would like to complete the following day that are in some way related to your long term goals. You don't need to go into huge detail. We have found that a card index box or diary is great for this. After listing your seven tasks, number them in order of importance as follows:

1, 2 or 3 MUST DO TODAY
4 or 5   WOULD LIKE TO DO TODAY
6 or 7   CAN WAIT UNTIL TOMORROW

 When you have done the job, cross or tick it off. If you don't manage to complete all your

Sue

I visited Nik and Eva at a time when I was running four small businesses. It's fair to say that my work/life balance was not ideal. I found it very difficult to "choose" to stop working and focus on the family and working from 7.00am to midnight had become the norm.

When I met the Speakmans I was immediately struck by their enthusiasm. I am by nature positive and enthusiastic, so it felt totally natural working with them and I liked the fact that their methods are unconventional. (If I had wanted conventional I wouldn't have opted for "A Life Coach Less Ordinary!") They were warm, friendly and absolutely right in their analysis of my situation which focused me on two specific things. The first was to get back into a routine of having a meal with the family. The second involved introducing "The Speakman Success Seven" into my life. Oh yes, and I also bought myself a trampoline. (Have you seen Eva's legs, they're amazing!)

Since meeting them I have taken on a part time assistant, sold one business, closed down the other two and focused on Party Crew (which was where my real ambitions and excitement were rooted). My business has gone from strength to strength. The relationships within the family have improved and I can choose to spend time with the family, rather than at my computer without feeling too guilty.

I am happy to count Nik and Eva as my friends, I love their views on life and I would much rather have one of their upbeat emails than listen to people who complain but aren't prepared to do anything about things. Life's too short and there's no excuse for not making changes to make it better.

tasks, add any that are outstanding to the next day's list. When you have completed the list put two diagonal lines through the entire card or page and write in the middle "ACHIEVED."

This approach keeps you focused on what's really important and stops daily mundane tasks from swamping your dreams. At the end of every day, you can also applaud yourself for what you have accomplished. There is no reason at all to dwell on what you haven't done, or what needs doing tomorrow as this will feature in tomorrow's list. Even if you only manage one thing on the list you are one step closer to achieving your ultimate ambitions.

We refer to our list of seven tasks every day to ensure that nothing is overlooked. The fantastic thing is when we look back at all the amazing things that we have achieved over the years this just motivates us to do even more stuff. It is a brilliant way to get your drive and momentum going!

4.

Beware of the passion killers

"Chase your **passion** not your pension."

Nik Speakman

"Nothing great in this world has ever been accomplished **without passion.**"

Georg W. Wegel

"**Passion** makes the difference between being **good** at something and being **outstanding.**"

Nik Speakman

86

Success is fuelled by passion

We've seen so many people who are doing a job they hate and have lost their optimism and sense of identity. But when they switch to a job they love, then they suddenly they come alive. They are confident, bursting with ideas and can't wait to get going every day. This is true passion. All the most successful people in life have it from sports stars to directors of massive corporations. Passion will keep you committed despite the setbacks. Passion will drive you on persistently despite rejection and failure. It is the fuel that makes us work hard and keeps us focused. Passion is one of the most important qualities that you can have if you want to succeed. (If you hadn't noticed, we've got the stuff in spades!) In fact, there's a great saying, "The three Ps of success are passion, persistence and patience."

Another great thing is that even though passion begins in the mind, it can have a brilliant effect on the body too. Your voice, your heart rate, your energy levels and even your posture all change when you are filled with enthusiasm. Passionate people are just far more enjoyable to be around and attract and generate zest and enthusiasm in others. So the more you radiate, you more you'll receive. It's a WIN WIN situation!!!

So be true to yourself!

FIND YOUR PASSION!!! EMBRACE IT!!! DRINK IT!!! BREATH IT!!! LIVE IT!!! BE IT!!!

are you **guilty** of
self sabotage?

Following your dream means facing your True Self. You need HUGE amount of courage and TONS of self-belief. Fear is the number one reason why people do not aim high. Fear of the unknown, fear of failure and paradoxically fear of success! Fearful people are scared to make a decision and would rather wait until they are 100% sure of the outcome, or for the decision to be made for them. Remember, you can only feel 100% sure of your outcome after you have got off your butt and achieved it.

You may feel comfortable with the familiar, but you will experience by far the greatest personal rewards when you do something to step out of your comfort zone. Moving away from the familiar is even harder if you also add zero self confidence, lack of self control, self-limiting labels and all other manner of negative thinking habits which may be conditioned programs that have been installed by family, friends, teachers and peer groups. Although consciously it sounds ridiculous, it never surprises us when we hear that someone still believes the things they were told by a classmate at primary school. Would you alter your whole life today if a nine year-old child were to tell you something? Probably not; yet this is what so many people are actually doing.

Negative emotions like anger, grief, shame, anxiety, sadness, guilt, regret and jealousy can all raise your blood pressure and unbalance your immune system, which can lead to strokes and heart attacks. But even before you get to that stage, you will experience a pretty poor quality of life. Alcohol, drugs, cigarettes and binge eating are just some of the ways people fill the void in their lives. So whatever personal demons are plaguing you, it's time to face up to them and KICK THEM OUT! You don't need them, they will drag you down. They will kill your motivation and eventually kill you!

Every behaviour, good and bad, is associated with a perception that it will produce a positive outcome in some way. For example, someone who drinks a bottle of red wine might associate it with the idea of better health (because it neutralises cholesterol?!). Someone who smokes may associate it with being cool and mixing with cool people. Eating chocolate might conjure up the idea of reward and so on...

Behaviours that have been learned can be unlearned. There is no such thing as addiction, only bad habits *and habits can be broken*. If you PASSIONATELY want to give up any of these habits you must start by telling yourself that from this day on "I am teetotal" "I am a non-smoker" or "I am able to control my eating habits."...Visualise yourself as this brilliant, healthy positive person, exploding with zest for life.

IF YOU CAN SEE IT, YOU CAN BE IT!

WATCH OUT FOR THE DREAM BUSTERS

Sadly, you may sometimes encounter people who want to put you in your place, wipe the smile off your face and bring you down to their level. The sad thing is, a few words from a dream buster can stop you in your tracks and kill your ambitions forever. So be prepared and be aware. You will probably hear one or more of the following comments as you start heading towards your goal.

What do you want to do that for?
You're just selfish and obsessed
Do you think you're better than everyone else?
You will never stick at it, you'll get bored
There are far better things to do in life than chasing a dream!

Unfortunately, we don't always realise the effect that the garbage people tell us has upon us. So beware. Before you start following your dreams you need to understand what you may come up against and why. People react to the prospect of success in one of two ways. They can be supportive and appreciative and feel inspired to do something themselves. Or, they can see it as a threat to their idea of the status quo.

Jealousy and resentment are common reactions towards someone who is wealthier, slimmer or happier say, than they are. These people view success as nothing more than a means of emphasising their own self-imposed limitations. Instead of emulating success, they ridicule it, criticise it and generally do all they can to make that person's life a misery. External negativity can be dealt with quite simply by physically moving away from it.

The real problems start however, when this negative garbage has been programmed into your unconscious and therefore it starts coming from your own head. Nothing kills a dream better than excuses like "I really couldn't..." "I don't have the time..." "If only things were different..." That's when you have to make a conscious effort to get to the root cause of these self doubts and delete the corrupted program. The key to making your unconscious mind supportive of your ambitions is to learn how you can control it.

> "Successful people use the bricks that others have thrown at them to build the foundations for their future."
>
> Eva Speakman

> "There are many close friends and family members who are 'Guilt Trip Travel Agents.' The great news is, we don't have to buy their tickets!"
>
> Nik Speakman

"Keep away from people who try to belittle your ambitions Small people always try to do that, but the really great make you feel that you too can become great."

Mark Twain

With friends like these...

The human body is full of and is surrounded by electric currents and electro-magnetic fields. In other words, ENERGY. This energy is constantly being picked up and shared by other people. That's why we sometimes say things like "He's not on my wavelength" or "She's giving me bad vibes." When you are trying to take yourself forward and bring happiness and success into your life, you would do well to think hard about your friends and what each of them means to you.

Once a year, we recommend that you make a list of everyone that you have come into contact with or spoken to on more than one occasion in the last month. This list can then be used as an acquaintance audit. This may sound ruthless but you should really consider what effect each of these human contacts is having on your life. We have discovered that people tend to fall into one of three categories: DRAGGERS, SUPPORTERS and IGNITERS.

You know what it's like to spend time with a dragger. The conversation is dull, often negative and there are very few laughs. The aim of a dragger is to make you experience their low energy levels and to understand how bad it feels to be them, so they can elicit your sympathy. They are called draggers because they literally drag you down. The longer you spend with these individuals the more your energy will be sapped away. You are best advised to say goodbye to these people, and the sooner the better. They are not interested in you, only in inflicting their pain upon you, or any other willing listener for that matter.

Supporters are brilliant. They cheer you on, tell you you're wonderful and make you feel good. They listen to you intently and almost always agree with your views. They are interested in you, care about you and make you feel valued. Although they don't really excite you or spark new ideas (your energy levels remain neutral), supporters are good people to know.

Your life is much better though, when you fill it with igniters. Igniters are people who make things happen. They go through life taking full responsibility for everything they do. They are alive with curiosity and they are open to new experiences. They are successful and creative and are continually looking at ways to make their lives better. When they find a great way of doing something they will tell you about it. When they see something they like about your life they will ask you all about it. Their energy is contagious and your energy levels are boosted. Igniters are interested in you and best of all, you are interested in them!

Igniters are great people. You should hang out with them and hang on to them!

"Call to mind the **deepest, darkest** and most negative truth about yourself and know this **truth** is a **lie.**"

Zen teaching

"What we think of **ourselves** defines the boundaries that limit our ideas of who we **believe we are** and who we believe we can **actually be.**"

Nik Speakman

OUR OWN WORST ENEMIES?

One of the hardest things for people to accept when they think about improving their lives is that *they themselves* are responsible for the way their life is now. As a grown adult our minds are full learned behaviors. All our thoughts, habits, the way we express ourselves, how we dress and what we say, is the result of a process of impressions that have been made upon us throughout our lives.

As we get older, we start contemplating what we have achieved and comparing it to the dreams we had when we were younger. At the age of around 40, we may even have what people refer to as a "mid-life crisis" and feel fed up, bored, adventurous or confused about what makes us happy. What we are doing is searching for our true selves, not the role we have assumed to please others. Then we may start to ask ourselves, "How on earth did this happen? Where did it all go wrong?"

To understand the situation you have to take a look at the way your mind is programmed from the day you are born. From zero to about the age of seven you unconsciously learn how people behave from your parents, or whoever is around you at the time. From the age of eight and 13, being eager to please, you adapt to those around you by consciously and unconsciously copying them. For example, you might have seen your friends biting their nails or smoking and tried it yourself, or start to copy the attitude of a favorite pop star. In the meantime, you may for example have also unconsciously developed an aversion to relationships because of your parent's own bad marriage or formed distorted views about yourself because of comments made about you at school. During the ages of 14 and 21 you learn how to socialise and form opinions about the way you relate to others. After that, you build upon what you've got, what you've experienced and what you have been influenced by.

The problem is, you can end up practicing the same harmful patterns of behaviour and running the same negative mental programs every day. Not only that, you even start embellishing them and reinforcing them, so they literally end up shaping your future. Whether it's the barrage of messages from the media, companies trying to sell us their products, images of "perfect" lifestyles or negative mental programming created when we younger, we tend to focus on all the things that we think are wrong with us. A lot of the time, other people cannot even see these so-called "faults" and are surprised to hear that we think so little of ourselves.

This is because everything that has ever happened to us in our lives has been processed and stored as a program in the mind. So when we come across any situation, our reaction to it is the result of a lifetime of these programs. What this means is that everyone sees the world in a slightly different way. What is an ugly, modern building to one person is a beautiful piece of modern architecture to another. A slice of chocolate cake covered in cherries may make one person's mouth water and another to feel sick. *It's all about perception and what people believe.*

Let's take this a stage further. There are women who consider themselves to be fat, whereas in fact, they are actually underweight. In bodybuilding culture, huge muscular men can look in the mirror and most amazingly see themselves as small. This phenomenon now even has a name: bigorexia! There are also people who think they are incredibly entertaining when they are drunk, but in reality they are just embarrassing.

Our thoughts can distort our perception of what is really happening. We all create our own reality and then fix it in our minds like a software program in a computer's hard drive. If it's run often enough it becomes our automatic default setting. Think about your beliefs. Practice self observation, not self analysis. Notice what you are doing and what you are saying then ask yourself WHY?

If you are telling yourself you are worthless, useless, unattractive, boring, ugly, always wrong...you are actually being the biggest bully to yourself and need to delete that program!

I CAN'T SING...run program...I'LL NEVER GET THAT JOB...run program...I CAN'T BE SUCCESSFUL...I AM WORTHLESS...I WILL NEVER DO THAT...run program...PEOPLE ARE NASTY...I CAN'T EVER BE HAPPY...NOONE CARES ABOUT ME...I AM LAZY...run program...IT'S ALWAYS ME...I CAN'T HELP IT...NOONE THINKS I CAN DO IT...I WILL NEVER BE ABLE TO DRIVE...run program...PEOPLE SHOULD BE NICER TO ME...I AM BORING...I AM UNPOPULAR...IT'S IMPOSSIBLE TO BE GOOD AT THIS...I AM A FAILURE...I AM AN IDIOT...I AM USELESS AT RELATIONSHIPS...run program...I CAN'T SUCCEED AT THIS...I AM UNATTRACTIVE...EVERYONE THINKS I AM DUMB...run program...I AM

"It is better to make the effort to light even the smallest candle than to just grumble about the darkness..."

Nik and Eva Speakman

Limiting beliefs

Limiting beliefs are like a stubborn stain. But with the correct stain remover and a bit of elbow grease, they can be erased! You can recognise a limiting belief from statements that start with:

"I can't…"
"I'll never…"
"Everyone thinks…"
"No one thinks…"
"People always…"
"People never…"

Other examples could be:

"I'm not coordinated."
"I can't maintain a long term relationship."
"People never listen to me."
"No one cares."
"Learning to play the piano is difficult."
"People are nasty."
"It's always me."
"They don't want…"
"It's a waste of time…"
"It's no good…"
"It's not for the likes of me."

Challenge your belief system

This exercise will help you replace limiting beliefs with more empowering, life enhancing beliefs. Whenever you use a statement like those above, practice the following:

STEP 1: CHALLENGE IT!
Ask yourself:
"Have I always believed this?"
"Where did this belief come from?"
"What evidence do I have to support this belief?"
"Have I believed this since childhood?"
"Is this belief still valid?"
"Who do I know who holds an opposite belief?"
"In what way is the belief ridiculous?"
"What evidence suggests this belief is untrue?"

STEP 2: REPLACE IT
Brainstorm for beliefs that open up more possibilities, that are more empowering, motivating and positive. Try various beliefs

until you find one that fits! State your new belief in the positive. For example:
"I *can* learn to play the piano and I am learning new things in each lesson."

STEP 3: PRACTICE IT
Integrate your new beliefs. Imagine how your life will improve when you have changed your beliefs. Imagine yourself using the new belief. Imagine having a conversation using your new belief. Ensure that the new belief feels good and makes you feel positive. If not, try others until you feel really good about yourself.

STEP 4: BE COMMITTED TO IT
Before finally committing to the new belief, consider how it might affect other people. If your new belief is lawful, motivating and will not only enhance your life but that of others too, then commit to it and practice it often.

PESSIMISTS ARE REALISTS (Yes, really!)

What we mean by this is if you expect the worst it will happen. Cynical people look at the whole world as if it's out to get them. They see optimists as naïve fools who are out of touch with reality. What they don't realise is this is only THEIR reality. Having spent their lives looking out for everything that supports their negative view, they are absolutely convinced that they are only ones that can see things as they really are.

Optimists are realists too. It just depends how you see things. Is your glass half full or is it half empty, smashed on the floor and staining the carpet? Let's take this a stage further and imagine the following situations:

The pessimist gets to work to find that a supplier has let him down and his warehouse manager has handed in his notice. He lets rip at the supplier thinking he must be completely incompetent and tells everyone that he never rated that warehouse manager anyway. Result: The supplier tells him to take his business elsewhere. Therefore the pessimist also loses his best customer and all his staff feel threatened and demoralised. He gets home to find that the garage door his son was supposed to have painted has still not been done. Before his son can say a word, he tells him he's useless and is always letting him down. He pours himself a large whisky. Result: his son is bitter and resentful and vows to leave home as soon as possible... and liver disease is one step closer.

The optimist gets to work and finds that a supplier has let him down and his warehouse manager has handed in his notice. He finds out what the supplier's problems are, explains the situation to the customer and tells them exactly when their goods will arrive. Result: the supplier gives him free stock with his next delivery, which he sends to his customer who later increases their business with him. He accepts the warehouse manager's notice and is quietly glad that he now has an opportunity to replace him with someone better. He gets home to find that the garage door his son was supposed to have painted has still not been done. He listens as his son explains that he has been ill in bed most of the day. He goes indoors and makes them both a cup of tea. Result: his son feels loved and valued and the cup of tea makes them both feel better.

Achievers have learned the right way to talk to themselves and others. They know what they want and how to modify their behaviour to get what they want. They are also very good at seeing opportunities in situations of adversity. Their subconscious default setting is constantly giving the message "It's okay... it's possible... I CAN DO IT!!!"

Another reason why pessimists are bad news...

Recently I stopped at a petrol station and after paying for the petrol, I decided to get a newspaper and a bottle of water. The young woman at the desk said, "That will be five pounds please." As I reached into my wallet it occurred to me that five pounds seemed a lot for a newspaper and a bottle of water. When I looked up, she had a big smile on her face. "Gotcha!" she said, "I've got to get my tip in there somehow!"

I laughed because I knew I'd been had. She then glanced down at the newspaper and said, "I'm sick and tired of all this negative stuff on the front pages. I want to read some good news for a change." She thanked me for coming in and said, "Maybe we'll get lucky tomorrow; maybe we'll get some good news!" That woman made my day. It's not that often that people I run into are so positive. Later that week I called in for more petrol (the benefits of driving a Hummer). I went to the same petrol station but this time a different young lady was behind the counter. I said, "Good afternoon" and handed her my money. She said nothing; not a word, not a smile. Nothing. She handed me my change and in a negative tone shouted "Next!"

Then it hit me right between the eyes: two people the same age; one had made me feel great and the other had made me feel lousy. By the choices we make, the way we think and the attitudes we exhibit, we can influence the lives of our family, our peers, our friends, and even strangers we've never met before.

So here is a challenge. Try and become that bubbly person who made me laugh and just watch how that changes the attitudes of people around you. Eva and I have made it a game now. Every time that we are out we have a competition to see who can get the most smiles from people we don't know. There's one point for making them smile and three points for making them laugh... and whoever gets the most points wins!

believe it
and live it!

Our belief has an immense impact on what happens. If you wake up and tell yourself you're going to have a miserable day, then you will. If you tell yourself that you are a loser and nothing good ever happens then you will go through life missing out on opportunities. Did you know you can also do the opposite? Some beliefs can set you free, while others will limit you and hold you back. By identifying what is stopping you from being open to new possibilities, you can literally turn your life around.

It was always considered impossible for any human being to be able to run a mile in under four minutes. Roger Bannister questioned this belief and with planning and determination and a clear goal in mind, he ran a mile in under four minutes because he firmly believed that it *was* possible. Everyone around him, including colleagues and journalists, advised him that it could not be done but Roger thought about it, practiced it and with the help of two friends who paced him throughout the challenge, he achieved it! Roger firmly believed that the human body was capable of reaching this goal and therefore he had total faith in himself and the outcome of his experiment.

The incredible thing was that as soon as he proved that it was possible to run a mile in under four minutes, many others managed to do the same thing. It is quite alarming to think that those who followed Roger's example had always been able to achieve this but had chosen to believe in everyone else's opinions and not in themselves.

Belief in a positive outcome can make that outcome a reality.

A stretch of the imagination...

Nik first saw this example at a seminar he attended in the early 1990s. It had such a great impact upon him that he began reading anything he could about visualising techniques. These have now become invaluable in the coaching methods that we use today.

1. Stand up and look directly ahead. Stretch your right arm straight out in front of you at shoulder height.

2. Keeping your feet firmly on the ground and not moving your pelvis at all, turn to your right arm in a circle and move it as far around to the back of your body as you can, keeping it level.

3. Notice the point that you reach and to what object or part of the room your fingers are pointing.

4. Now close your eyes and with your arm outstretched, imagine that you are repeating the above, but are moving further round and past the point you previously reached with ease.

5. Repeat this twice more, while imagining you are effortlessly almost managing to turn 360 degrees.

6. Now open your eyes and try the exercise again. You will be able to reach much further around than the first time you tried.

As in life... you are capable of achieving things you never thought possible when you abandon your self-limiting beliefs.

"If you believe you can, you probably can. If you believe you won't, you most assuredly won't. Belief is the ignition switch that gets you off the launching pad."

Denis Waitley

let your unconscious mind do all the hard work!

As we said before, the mind is very similar to a computer. The conscious mind is like the RAM, which has little storage space in comparison to the unconscious mind which is like the hard drive and has enormous storage space. It is therefore very important that we transfer skills over from our conscious mind, which has relatively limited space, to our unconscious mind. To do this, we must pass through four learning stages:

1 **Unconscious incompetence** means that you are unconsciously unaware of what you want to do and therefore you have no clue whether you are incompetent and able to do it or not. This situation would apply to anyone who wasn't happy with their life but just had accepted it as being their lot.

2 **Conscious incompetence** is when you consciously realise that there is something that you want to learn about or change but you are incompetent or not sure how to do it. For example, as you are reading this book, you know that life can be how you want it, but right now you are not exactly sure how to change it. This learning step can prove more frustrating than the first as you have just discovered something that you currently cannot do.

3 **Conscious competence** is when you know consciously what you want to achieve and also that when you do it you are competent at it, like remembering to be positive for example, which is fantastic. The only problem is that you have to remind yourself to *competently* do it. The drawback with this is that our conscious mind can only cope with so much. If you are working, drinking a cup of tea, thinking about what you did last night, thinking about your problems and someone is distracting you with their conversation and all the time you are trying to remind yourself to stay positive, your brain could start to get rather overloaded!

Unconscious competence is where you need to be!

This is when your unconscious mind can do what you want competently without you having to do a thing about it! You will all know by now that Eva and I have a passion for cars. Imagine therefore, how important it was for me to be able to drive. Wow, it was as if my life depended on it! However, my first lesson (conscious incompetence) was a disaster. My brain went into overload. How could I be expected to turn the steering wheel with both hands then take one off to change gears whilst simultaneously pressing the clutch and putting my other foot on the accelerator whilst keeping it ready to cover the brake in addition to watching where I was driving AND looking in three mirrors at once. Aaaarrrghhh!

I remember thinking that I would NEVER be able to drive. This was a great example of progression for me because I then looked at people getting in and out of their cars and compared myself to them. I found myself saying, "What am I talking about? If they can do it so can I!" In fact, we now use the term POSSIBLE IN THE WORLD THEN POSSIBLE FOR ME! Please believe us that this statement can relate to anything. Needless to say I passed my test and am now unconsciously competent at driving. So much so that some years ago I remember driving one of my cars while speaking on my cell phone, drinking a bottle of water and steering with my knees!!!

I am sure that you will have experienced something that you thought you could never do and yet now you do it without hesitation and virtually without thinking.

"We dare to teach because we continue to learn."

Nik and Eva Speakman

"Every act of conscious learning requires the willingness to suffer an injury to one's self-esteem. That is why young children, before they are aware of their own self-importance, learn so easily."

Thomas Szasz

Inspiring lives...

If ever anyone has beaten the odds it is Lance Armstrong. As the best cyclist in the world, his achievements are already off the scale. But when you consider that his greatest sporting triumphs came AFTER he was diagnosed with cancer, Lance Armstrong is nothing less than a breathtaking phenomenon. His story is so remarkable it beats my recovery from ulcerative colitis hands down! That for me, is just one of the reasons why he is such a hero.

His story is so remarkable it's almost unreal. How on earth could anyone overcome such a devastating diagnosis, have his body burned from the inside out, undergo surgeries and not only recover, but go on to win the Tour de France an amazing seven times in a row? If you ever need to be reminded of the power of human spirit and how focus and belief can surpass the most crippling of obstacles in life, read about his journey. He has taken human strength and concentrated it with such intensity that he turned himself into a powerhouse of positive energy! His accomplishments are simply incredible.

Lance's mother Linda was just 17 when she gave birth to him in Dallas in Texas in 1971. Two years later, his father abandoned them both and Lance never saw him again. Linda then married Terry Armstrong, a preacher who talked a lot about religion but would beat Lance with a boat paddle. Not surprisingly, Lance was glad when he also decided to walk out. His mother took on several jobs and thanks to her hard work, Lance never wanted for anything. (He later credited his mother for teaching him the work ethic which enabled him to win the Tour de France.)

At the age of 12, Lance wanted to be a football player. But as he lacked coordination he began taking part in triathlons. This involved swimming, running and cycling. His morning workout started at 5.30 am and went through until 7.00 am. He also rode 20 miles to swimming practice on his bike before sunrise. At 13 years old he became a junior triathlon athlete and went on to win so many races that he made $20,000 in one year!

In 1987, aged 16, he was also winning bicycle races. He was asked to attend the

Cooper Institute in Dallas for tests. Lance was assessed for his aerobic ability, i.e. the maximum amount of oxygen his lungs could consume during exercise. His levels were the highest ever recorded at the clinic. His body also seemed to be specially constructed for cycling. For example, his long thigh bones enabled him to apply just the right amount of torque to the pedals. In other words, he was a natural.

In his senior year of high school the US Cycling Federation invited Lance to enter the 1990 Junior World Championships in Moscow. Although he didn't win, he was accepted by the US national cycling team and went to Europe to train. Lance entered the biggest race in Italy. All the best pros in the country were there and an American had never beaten them before. Nobody believed Lance had a chance but he surprised them all by winning. This made him think that maybe he had could win the Tour de France, a huge 2,000 mile one-lap race around the entire country.

Lance went on to win the US Amateur Cycling Championship in 1991 and turned professional the following year. By 1996 he had a contract worth two million dollars with a French cycling team, a beautiful new home in Austin, Texas and a Porsche that he liked to drive fast!

Later that year he became unusually weak and felt soreness in one of his testicles. But as soreness was a part of a cyclist's life, he didn't give it much thought. But just days after his 25th birthday the symptoms became more disturbing. First, he felt something metallic in his throat while he was talking on the phone. He put his friend on hold and ran to the bathroom and coughed into the sink, which became splattered with blood. Soon after this, Lance was diagnosed with testicular cancer. (Incredibly, he now refers to this moment as the best thing that ever happened to him.)

The malignant testicle was removed and the surgery was successful. However, a. CT-scan revealed that the condition had spread into his lungs, abdomen and even his brain. It had reached a fairly advanced stage because he had waited so long before seeking help. The doctors told him he had a 50/50 chance of surviving. (Actually his odds were much worse, but they did not want to get his spirits down.)

He needed brain surgery and the most aggressive type of chemotherapy. At that point, he only had a slim chance of living another year. One of the doctors that treated Lance described him as "the most willful person I have ever met and he wasn't willing to die!" Lance underwent four rounds of chemotherapy that was so powerful that it destroyed his muscles and caused permanent kidney damage. The chemicals also burnt his skin from the inside out. The French cycling team that Lance had recently joined was convinced that his career (and probably his life) was over. So while Lance was in hospital they told his agent that they wanted to reconsider the terms of his contract.

Lance underwent chemotherapy for several months. He vowed that once he had beaten the disease he would become a spokesperson to increase awareness of the illness and raise funds for research and new treatments. He knew that had he been more aware of what the symptoms meant he would have consulted a doctor much sooner. He could not stand the thought that someone else might suffer the same fate.

The chemotherapy and surgery made him weak and nauseous and all his hair fell out. Eventually, after several arduous months of treatment, the doctors told him that he had beaten the disease. A month after his last chemotherapy session, he met Kristin Richard who worked with him on his foundation, "Ride for Roses." She was to eventually become his wife and later gave birth to three children with sperm that had been frozen before his treatment began.

The therapy had made Lance so weak that he could hardly ride his bicycle around the block. As a bike racer before his illness, Lance won races because he was confident that noone could beat him. He would stand on the starting line, look at the other racers and say to

104

himself, "I am the strongest, smartest, most prepared rider in this race. I can win today." As a cancer survivor, his body was a shadow of what it had been. The experience had also made him less confident of his ability.

His first attempts to return to competition ended in exhaustion and depression. Each time Lance decided to make a more serious effort to return to racing he felt like giving up. He came 14th in the Ruta del Sol which is a five-day race held each year in Spain. He had never done better even before having cancer, yet he still felt like quitting. But his coaches helped to persuade him that this wasn't the way to end his career, so Lance agreed to prepare for one last event in the USA. It was over 100 miles up a mountain. Along the course he suddenly left his partner and started racing. Cycling in sleet and snow, Lance was attacking the mountain as if he was in the Tour de France. When he got up to the top of the peak his coach told him to load the bike on the car so they could go home. But Lance said, "Give me my rain jacket I'm riding back."

This was the moment that Lance finally regained his strength and rediscovered the joy he felt riding a bicycle. He decided that winning the biggest race in the world was the best thing he could do for other people dealing with cancer. So he began training for the next Tour with incredible commitment and focus. He didn't miss workouts, he was careful about what he ate and he got plenty of sleep, going to bed at around 8.00 pm.

In 1999 he qualified for the Tour. However, most of the teams didn't want to include him because they didn't believe he really was cured of his cancer. Eventually though, he was accepted by the US Postal Cycling Team. He practiced every day, even in sub-zero temperatures because he knew that to win he needed to be familiar with every condition and the Alps were part of the race. So he practiced biking up mountains when it was snowing, such was his determination to be ready for the race.

In the Tour de France each day is called a "stage." There are 24 stages in the race and the winner of the stage gets to wear a yellow jersey. The ride up the Alps was most difficult and many of the best cyclists gave up. But with the help of his teammates, Lance

© Carl W. Southerland

"Anything is possible. You can be told that you have a 90% chance or a 50% chance or a 1% chance... But you have to believe and you have to fight."

Lance Armstrong

won this stage and went on to cross the finishing line in Paris and won the Tour de France.

Lance then decided to enter the Tour de France the following year and won it again in 2000. He entered the Tour in 2001 and won again and did the same thing the year after that. 2003 was his hardest Tour by far. Lance described it as one of the most gruelling and painful experiences of his career. He literally wanted to step off the bike. But he didn't. Instead, he went on to dominate cycling's biggest event, winning the race seven times in a row from 1999 through 2005.

The physical demands on competitive cyclists are immense. The Tour de France has been described as the equivalent of running twenty marathons in twenty days. On average, the cyclists burn between 6,500 and 10,000 calories a day for three weeks. (Active people might use as many as 3,500). The cyclists can also race at speeds of up to 50 mph and when they crash (which is often) it can result in broken bones and the smell of burning flesh. Yet they will pick themselves up and keep going, sometimes when they are seriously injured. "Cycling is so hard," said Lance in his autobiography, "the suffering is so intense, that it's absolutely cleansing. The pain is so deep and strong that a curtain descends over your brain..."

Early in his career Lance only had average muscle efficiency. Incredibly, he managed to increase it by 8% through hard and dedicated training. However, Lance also had some great genetic advantages that helped become the greatest cyclist in the world. His muscles produced about half as much lactic acid than average when they got fatigued. So he could recover much faster than other people. His heart is almost a third larger than that of an average man and can beat over 200 times a minute when he exerts himself. This means that huge volumes of blood and oxygen could be pumped to his legs. By contrast, his resting heart rate is just 32 beats a minute which is so slow that a doctor who didn't know him would probably call a hospital as soon as he heard it!

Sadly, because Lance is the best cyclist in the world, there was an assumption that he must use drugs. Yet he never failed a drug test despite the fact that he has probably been the most frequently examined athlete in the history of sport! Whenever he won a day's stage, or finished as one of the top cyclists in a longer race, he was required to provide a urine sample. The skeptics could not believe that he could be so successful without drugs. According to his coach the advantage that he had was that he simply worked harder than anyone else alive.

As mentioned previously, Lance said that cancer was the best thing that ever happened to him. Before becoming ill, he didn't care about strategy or tactics or teamwork. For example, in the 1993 Tour he didn't even finish the race. He dropped out when the teams entered the mountain phase in the Alps. He also failed to finish in 1994 and 1996. Before the disease struck him he didn't train properly and just relied on his gift. When he came back, he just went into a different zone and trained far more than his competitors.

Lance won a personal victory by beating his own cancer. It was also a victory for all cancer patients when he won the Tour de France so many times after beating the disease. He now campaigns for more government funds for cancer research and treatment and through the Lance Armstrong Foundation, inspires and empowers others facing the same situation as he once did.

Lance Armstrong has shown the world that the most feared of diseases does not have to be the end; it can be the birth of new, productive and happy life.

To visit the Lance Armstrong Livestrong Foundation go to:
http://www.livestrong.org
Donations can be made online or by contacting donations@laf.org.

"We are so much stronger than we imagine, and belief is one of the most valiant and long-lived human characteristics. To believe, when all along we humans know that nothing can cure the briefness of this life, that there is no remedy for our basic mortality, that is a form of bravery...

Without belief, we would be left with nothing but an overwhelming doom every single day. And it will beat you. I didn't fully see, until the cancer, how we fight every day against the creeping negatives of the world, how we struggle daily against the slow lapping of cynicism.

Dispiritedness and disappointment, these are the real perils of life, not some sudden illness or cataclysmic millennium doomsday. I know now why people fear cancer. It is a slow and inevitable death; it is the very definition of cynicism and loss of spirit."

Lance Armstrong

5.

Thinking therapy

Our brain is just like a computer

We have realised that the human brain is just too magnificent to fully appreciate. Please bear in mind that anything in this world that exists beyond nature started as an idea in the mind first. To explain to our clients exactly what it is capable of, we like to compare the brain with a computer. We reiterate time and time again within our sessions that when we are born our brain is void of information. Just like a new computer, no software has been loaded and therefore there are no programs to access. (For those who are unfamiliar with computers, another analogy we use is that the brain is like an empty juke box which has no records installed yet.)

Many people say to us, "I was born with a temper." Or, "I must have been born with my phobia," or "I grew up being shy" and so on. NOT SO! Virtually everything you do, say and believe: your quirks, your phobias and analogies have all been learned and then placed as a program (or disc) into your computer (or juke box!).

Your programs comprise things you have seen, heard, experienced, smelled, tasted and touched. The language you speak is that of the people who raised you and who surrounded you. You may have been born in a different country and moved to the UK when you were a baby, but you will speak English. Likewise, an English baby brought up in Spain would speak Spanish. You know not to touch something hot as you either had that program installed by your parents or you touched something hot and burnt yourself and installed your own program.

Once formed, a program or belief has the capacity for amazing consistency and accuracy in creating the same results repeatedly. (For example, with a phobia every time an arachnophobe sees a spider the same reaction occurs.) Some programs will enhance your life but others will be undesirable. This is where our techniques of reprogramming are a great help.

Phobias are usually created by something you saw or an event that occurred in your life. Limiting beliefs are often the result of something that you were told or heard. You are NOT born with a phobia or a limiting belief! You are NOT born lacking confidence, overweight, aggressive or unhappy. These conditions are a result of one or more undesirable programs running in your head. You are simply opting for a dysfunctional or limiting file from a computer database that YOU or someone around you installed! Phobias and reactions are caused by triggers to the unconscious mind that are accessed in just the same way that a computer mouse clicks on a program's icon. The trigger could be something you see, hear, feel, taste or smell.

The fantastic news is that any program can be deleted, amended or destroyed. You may have one brain but you have two minds: the conscious mind and the unconscious mind. Just like the computer has a limited amount of RAM memory to run some programs (like the conscious mind) it also has a huge hard drive with fantastic storage space similar to the unconscious mind. From the second you wake up you immediately start running programs in your unconscious mind. These are your habitual skills and they enable you to do things automatically like getting dressed, making breakfast *and* feeling good or feeling bad.

Although the two minds work cooperatively, the storage in the unconscious mind is far larger. So to help achieve the life you want, you need as many fantastic programs running in your unconscious mind as possible. *Remember, once created they have an amazing capacity for consistency.*

Also, if you run all your programs in your conscious mind you will feel overloaded. So you need to switch them over to your unconscious. The best way to do this is to make them a habitual skill by knowledge and repetition as four learning steps that follow demonstrate. You are currently reading this book with your conscious mind. However if while reading you suddenly drift, you may find yourself at the bottom of the page and wonder how you got there! The moment you started to drift the unconscious mind took over.

Successful people are often thought of as being lucky. Once again, there is no such thing as luck! *Luck is a personal choice* and it is created by taking control of your thinking, making an effort, taking action and installing positive programs. Luck is when preparation meets opportunity.

So be ready! Be prepared... and hold on to your pants while you shout it again... "WORLD I'M HERE!"

recognising your **true** reflection

We believe that a picture is worth a thousand words, but a metaphor is worth a thousand pictures. That's why our therapies draw strongly on the use of visual metaphors which we convey with the use of various props and effects. (To drive the message home we sometimes get involved in the process ourselves with dressing up and role playing as you may have seen!) One of our most effective therapies involves a large cheval mirror, which acts to give the person who is standing in front of it a true reflection of their inner self. We call it the ultimate reality check.

When clients stand in front of the mirror we expose their true inner voice by asking them to tell us exactly what they see. That's when we hear the negative internal commentary that they are telling themselves every single day. As they talk, we take a note everything they are saying and when they have finished, we read back their catalogue of put downs and insults. Most people are horrified and feel terrible at this point. It may sound extremely unpleasant, if not cruel, but remember, these are the person's own thoughts that are battering away at their spirit every day. When they burst into tears or start getting angry, they are reacting outwardly to their internal messages instead of enduring them in painful silence.

"A picture is worth a thousand words, but a metaphor is worth a thousand pictures."

Anon

Then we ask them to imagine that a person they love like their husband, child or mother or even a stranger told them they were fat, ugly, pathetic, a loser or any other defamatory statement they have said to themselves. What would they think? Would that be acceptable? How would it make them feel? We explain that they would not accept this kind of abuse from anyone else yet they accept it from themselves virtually every minute of the day. How disrespectful is that? It is not acceptable. It is rude, bad mannered and it is not right. Nobody should be that horrible to themselves.

Finally, with their eyes closed, we ask them to think about someone who loves them unconditionally, without exception, someone who loves them for who they are inside. They are told to imagine that this loving person is standing in front them and looking at them with love. We then ask them to float in to that person's body to give our client the opportunity of seeing themselves through the eyes of love. When we ask them to feel the love that is being projected, these positive, caring messages take the place of the harmful self destructive ones and create the right mindset for the affirmations that we then ask them to repeat: "I am a unique human being... I accept myself... I deserve a fantastic life... I respect myself..."

When these words are said with passion and belief, it releases them from their hurtful inner voice and puts them in touch with a new, far more appreciative one. For the first time, people see new, positive qualities in themselves. We then ask them to close their eyes and imagine they are looking at the person they want to become, proud, happy, confident and to step into the mirror and feel how it feels to be that person. After the count of three, they pull that person inside themselves.

This intense form of therapy has been likened to subjecting people to a whirlwind of emotions. But using the mirror we are often able to achieve the complete removal of self destructive ideas and replace them with wonderful thoughts that build self respect and self confidence.

"I accept myself...
I am a **unique**
human being"

Yasmin

At the age of thirty five, I had managed to pay back £37,000 worth of personal debt: a debt created by shopping. Having cleared all of my debts, anyone would think I would have learnt my lesson, but I knew that I was still a shopaholic and could easily slip back into my familiar habits.

My massive debts had built up over fifteen years, beginning in my twenties which was a time of just spend, spend, and spend some more. I would buy stuff for me and presents for friends, things for my home, meals out and holidays away. I bought things I don't even own now. I shopped when I was sad and when I was happy. I really did know the meaning of retail therapy!

Luckily, shortly after I had settled my debts I was introduced to Nik and Eva Speakman, the well known celebrity life coaches. I was not proud of my debt (not that long ago £37,000 could buy a small house!) but the Speakmans showed me not to be ashamed to face up to it. I have to say that their therapies were an odd blend of anger-inducing, sadness-inducing, laughter-inducing treatments. Little did I know I would be throwing bricks into a river and releasing myself from my "baggage," or standing in front of a mirror while Eva made me cry by telling me I was special and unique.

With Nik's kind, paternal voice sharing his many wise insights with me, the Speakmans really did "tell me what I needed to hear" (as is their motto) but in a caring and very nurturing way. They made me realise that I was trying to compensate for the death of my mother when I was just eight years-old and the endless shopping was a way of giving myself treats to reassure myself emotionally.

I learned that the old me was far too extravagant and generous. Nik and Eva taught me patience, restraint and balance. I can now walk away instead of buying something. As Eva impressed upon me, I am unique and I love myself. I now have self esteem and so there is no need to buy something to fill an emotional gap. Nik and Eva made me realise that I can be confident without needing to spend vast amounts of money constantly. They gave me permission to feel beautiful inside and to accept myself.

In the past, some of my worst purchases were always the little things bought in a hurry. Now there are no impulse buys. I may browse a little, but I often walk away without buying anything as the feeling of excitement, the "buzz" (which was removed with therapy) has gone.

After my visits to the Speakmans, I even developed a strong aversion to those string handled gift bags from expensive shops. I now hate (and I mean H-A-T-E) carrying them! This

could be to do with the fact that I had to carry six of them containing solid concrete bricks up a very steep hill. This painful exercise made me understand just how crippling the burden of my debts really had been. I figured that every bag was worth over £6,000 of debt. Boy, it certainly felt like it! Afterwards I had bruises on my shoulders! Eva was so concerned for me carrying those heavy bags and was almost in tears, she was so sweet.

I hope my story gives you inspiration and abundance. For any problem, there is always a solution if you look for it and ask for help. Nik and Eva taught me that the luxury of my life is on the inside not the outside. Life is about simplicity for me now. The Speakmans slowed me down and helped me find an inner discipline which I lacked. I now have no unsecured debt and I have promised myself to never own a credit card, or get an unsecured loan, hire purchase or store card again.

Nik and Eva have changed my life and helped me to heal. I now feel like the wealthiest woman in the world. Now all I owe is my gratitude to them.

"The best type of spending is that of spending time on one's own true happiness and fulfillment."

Eva Speakman

"Spending time developing your passion will make you incredibly rich."

Nik Speakman

115

If I could turn back time...

It is a fact that people who are nearing death do not look back and regret the things that they *have* done. They only regret the things they HAVEN'T done. At the end of your life your can either look back and wish you had summoned the courage to pursue your ambitions... Or you can start planning *now* to do all the things that you dreamed of so there are no regrets. You only walk upon this earth once. As long as you have time and energy you can live your dreams. Only YOU know what you want from your life and what will make you happy.

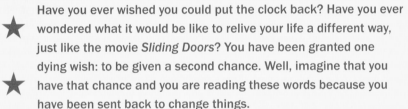

★ Rocking chair therapy ★

Have you ever wished you could put the clock back? Have you ever wondered what it would be like to relive your life a different way, just like the movie *Sliding Doors*? You have been granted one dying wish: to be given a second chance. Well, imagine that you have that chance and you are reading these words because you have been sent back to change things.

Find yourself a quiet room and sit down, preferably in a rocking chair. Close your eyes begin to rock back and forth and visualise yourself many years from now. How would you look? Think about how someone old sits, bent over and frail. Your muscles are tired, your breath is shallow and you feel weak. Reflect upon your life and think about the desires you had when you were young, the things you should have done differently... the things you always dreamed of... wanted to be... wanted to do... wanted to say... the places you wanted to visit... What do you regret? What were you good at and what could you have shared but held it back through fear? Think about those hopes and those dreams... Let your imagination take over... give your conscious voice a rest. It may be a surprise to discover the real you.

How rocking chair therapy worked for Nik...

My life felt perfect and I thought I knew all of my remaining goals. So when Eva suggested I try rocking chair therapy to see if I'd missed anything I agreed, thinking there couldn't possibly be anything I'd overlooked. It wasn't until I was aged 105 looking back on my life, that I discovered many things I wanted to do that were not on my goals list. Wow, swimming with great white sharks? I was amazed I would consider such a feat. Yet there it was a strong regret that I had never done it. So please reconfirm your goals with this fantastic exercise.

...and why Simon put his head in the clouds!

Simon came to see us because he had reached his 50s and felt quite hopeless about his future. All he seemed to do was work. He had no time for holidays, saw little of his wife and felt that his only purpose in life was to pay the bills. When he was asked what it was he wanted from life he could not answer. All he knew was what he didn't want. "I don't want to work all my life... I don't want to miss out on my family... I don't want to be tired all the time..."

We asked him to sit in the rocking chair and imagine himself as a very old man, bent and frail. Then we asked him to switch off and let his mind wander to search out all those long lost hopes and aspirations. When he eventually opened his eyes and looked at the sheet of paper on which we had been keeping notes he could not believe what he was reading.

One of the ideas that he had been excited about was travelling in a hot air balloon. A few days later he saw an advertisement for evening balloon champagne trips and booked his first ever hot air balloon ride with his wife. (This phenomenon, where something just falls into place, is based on the fact that whatever we think about most will happen as we acquire a new focus and direction that is guided by our subconscious mind. This occurrence is known as Reticular Activation. For example, when you buy a new car, you may notice everyone is driving the same model. The fact is, they were always out there but you just hadn't tuned in to them.)

Simon also told us that he wanted to spend more time with his wife and daughter. So we advised him to get a diary and block off the weeks that he would not be working and to start planning his trips abroad. With just a few simple steps, Simon made some major changes in his life and rediscovered dreams and ambitions that were in danger of being lost forever.

THE BEST WAY TO PREDICT YOUR FUTURE IS TO CREATE IT!

Having one of the De Loreans from the brilliant film *Back to The Future* provides us with a fantastic metaphor for "Time Line Therapy," which we use to great effect. To enhance the magic of the situation, we paint a time line on the ground and we even wear protective clothing, just as they did in the movie! The more the senses are involved in any therapy the more authentic the experience and the better it works.

We can take people back into the past and if they have any bad memories or regrets or forgiveness issues, they can deal with them. This frees them up to move on. We can also transport people into the future to show them what it could be like depending on the actions they take now.

This can be the worst 15 to 20 minutes of a person's life as they have to go back to when they experienced the most intense sorrow or pain, or we can take them forward to make them think about the effects the way they are living now will affect others as well as themselves if they don't do something to change things IMMEDIATELY. It can also be the best 15 to 20 minutes, because they will have the chance to see the person they can become and experience the joy of knowing their dreams were realised after all. When they emerge after this revelation, the tears are not of sorrow but of relief and joy.

"The future exists nowhere except in our thoughts."

Buddha

Robert

I was admitted into the care when I was seven years-old owing to my mother's ill health, (she suffered a nervous breakdown and had manic depression). During this part of my life I always tried to look to the future and dreamed of the day when I could be free to live my life as I wanted. After much determination and proving to the authorities that I could fend for myself, I eventually left the care system at the age of 16.

I have since constantly tried to put my past behind me but the emotional trauma I suffered as a result of mental abuse and bullying during my years in care was so deeply ingrained that I found this impossible. Over the years I have tried many ways to overcome my psychological issues of lack of confidence and anxiety without success. But then I saw the first series of 'A Life Coach Less Ordinary' and later noticed an advertisement on the UKTV website inviting people to take part in the second series. I applied immediately but did not expect to hear anything. Having had much bad luck in life, I felt that things like this just didn't happen to me. To my amazement, I was contacted and was asked to take part in the show.

Throughout my time with Nik and Eva, I was made to feel valued and special, something I had not felt for a very long time. They both had a natural and genuine warmth about them which helped put me at ease. I had several personalised treatments for my issues. These were very visual and cleverly designed to be unforgettable. Some seemed bizarre, but I told myself to keep an open mind and to just go with it. There were two in particular that really stood out for me. The first was when Nik, Eva and I stamped mud into a doormat with a photograph of my face stuck to it. It was then soaked in fuel and I set it alight. I watched it burn completely. This symbolised the end of years of feeling like a doormat with people walking over me.

One of my all-time favourite films is 'Back to the Future' as I have always loved the idea of being able to travel back in time and change the past (although I never mentioned this to anybody). This is why my second treatment really blew my mind! I sat in the original De Lorean car that was used in the movie! I closed my eyes and imagined travelling back to various traumatic times in my past. I then hugged and reassured the imaginary me at different ages of my childhood and told him that things would be alright.

Since seeing Nik and Eva, the pain I felt as a child is very much less severe. The main thought I have taken away with me is that if something in life makes you unhappy and is preventing you from going forwards, you must try to change it. I have put this into practice and have gradually seen changes starting to happen.

We have all had relationships with people in the past that if we don't let go of, will hold us back from our future. In addition, we have all said things in the heat of the moment that we regret afterwards. Yet we can sometimes be too stubborn to make amends and a friendship or a close relationship may consciously end. In either event, sometimes the unconscious mind keeps a link open which will cause emotional pain. Nik and I have both done this exercise and were surprised how many ties had been cut consciously but not unconsciously. But then again if you think of how many people we get to know over a lifetime it may not surprise you.

The following exercise is particularly beneficial when trying to move forward from a broken relationship or a situation with someone that is not is not beneficial to you (for example, a friend or family member that you have consciously chosen to move away from but your subconscious is not quite letting go).

★ Cutting ties exercise

1. Bring to mind the most vivid event you can that involves the person that you need to distance yourself from. When remembering the experience, envisage it with as much clarity as you can, noticing what you saw, smelled, heard and felt.

2. Focus on the person in that memory and notice too if you are seeing the memory through your eyes or that of a bystander. If you are a bystander in the memory then as you need to look through your own eyes you may want to choose another memory. Or you can imagine yourself floating into your body so that you are then looking out of your eyes.

3. Now look up and down the person for the link between you both. For example, it could be a ribbon, a cord, or string. The link may be attached to any part of their body and linked to a different part of yours such as the stomach, hand, forehead, foot etc.

4. Look at the person and thank them for the positive impressions they have made on you. If there are only negatives, thank them for making you realise that you no longer want that negativity in your life. Tell them they are no longer needed and say goodbye to them.

5. Now imagine you are holding a cutting implement in your hand, such as a sharp knife, a saw or a pair of scissors. With a physical cutting action you can then finally cut the tie.

6. Once you have cut through the attachment you may see a variety of things. Most commonly our clients see the person they have rid themselves of disappear like a balloon with the air escaping, vanishing in a puff of smoke or just smiling and walking away.

7. When they have disappeared, turn the opposite way to face your future. Slowly open your eyes, smile and walk forwards and away from your past.

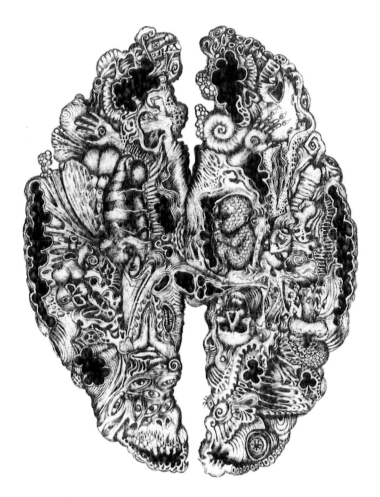

"A mind is its own place
and in itself, can make
a Heaven of Hell,
a Hell of Heaven."

John Milton,
Quotation from "Paradise Lost"

"Whatever you carry **on the inside** you can **get rid of...** throw it away... **burn it...** **shower it off...** run it over with a bulldozer... **whatever it takes!!!**"

Eva Speakman

Another approach that our clients find very liberating is to physically destroy the negative elements or harmful memories and associations that are plaguing their lives. We have been known to hire road rollers to literally crush bad influences. (In one example that was shown on TV it was alcohol and junk food). Or, we could take the client into the shower (wearing waterproofs of course) ask them to close their eyes and imagine the "dirt" that has stuck to them from past insults is being washed away. And when someone writes down their innermost fears and anxieties and then sees them go up in flames, a huge weight is also lifted from their shoulders.

Box and burn therapy

1. Write a list of everything in your life that has hurt or affected you negatively in some way. Use as many sheets of paper as you like. Include things that people have said to you, situations that have embarrassed or humiliated you and all of the bad things you think about yourself. Think about all the derogatory labels that you have given yourself and write them all down...just let all your darkest thoughts flood out onto the paper. Dump it all down in writing and don't stop until you have thought of everything that triggers any uncomfortable feelings, saddens or disappoints you. Go right back to your earliest memories and list every painful incidence that you can still remember. You are creating the opposite of a diary to keep to remind yourself how great your life was. **This is a diary that you will NEVER EVER have to refer to again.**

2. Do you still keep reminders of any of these situations, events or people in your house? If so, find any related materials such as photos, clothes, gifts, books and letters and put them in the box too. It amazes us how many people hold on to keepsakes (such as cuddly toys) from a previous relationship even when they are in a new one! If any of the items are too valuable to burn put them out of sight until you have sold them or given them away.

3. Take the box outside and burn it safely. As you watch all those harmful thoughts and memories go up in flames, firstly see the memories, then close your eyes and focus on their colours. As you concentrate on the colours of the memories in your mind, open your eyes and watch them gradually fade to white as they are consumed by the flames. (This sometimes happens when a photograph burns and the chemicals mix in the heat.) Feel the release as you end up seeing nothing but clear, crisp, pure white. Then say, "Goodbye forever... you can never come back... I am better off without you... I am free... I am strong and your hold on me is now over."

4. When the fire has died down and there is nothing left but cold, grey ashes, shovel up what is left, put it in a bin liner and throw it away. You never want to see any more reminders of the things that have hurt you in the past.

5. Repeat this exercise once a year, or whenever you feel yourself being dragged down by painful recurring thoughts. Remember, fire in nature is not just about death and destruction. It clears away dead wood and choking undergrowth, creates nutrients and enables new seeds to grow in the sunlight. Fire is nature's way of burning away the diseased and old to make way for a healthier new future. And it will do exactly the same thing for you too.

"We can't solve problems **by using** the same kind of thinking we used when **we created them.**"

Albert Einstein

"Your life is a reflection of **your mind.** Change your mind... **change your life!!!**"

Nik Speakman

Tackling the following emotional problems often requires the help of a qualified professional. These issues are entrenched in the mind and can dominate and ruin people's lives.

OBSESSIONS

An obsession is a *learned* behaviour. It is not genetically inherited. Nobody is born with an obsession. It is learnt by doing something repeatedly and then gradually adding new rules and bigger targets. This is all then programmed into the subconscious. It is at this point that an obsession can take on a life of its own and dominate every waking moment to the virtual exclusion of everything and everyone else.

To rid someone of an obsession we first identify the positive feelings that are associated with it and then change them to negative ones. In other words, we shift the balance away from pleasure and towards pain. For example, we would tell someone to think about someone that means more to them than their all-consuming habit. We would then take them into the future and make them look back and see how they would feel if they continued putting their obsession first. To intensify this thought, we sometimes use visual props to make these thoughts register deep in the subconscious.

For example, we successfully treated a woman with a 33-year old cleaning obsession by asking her the question, "What would happen to you and your loved ones if you don't change this obsession now?" By doing this, we managed to link tremendous pain and tragedy to her obsession. In other words, we shifted the balance of pain and pleasure and made the obsession seem hugely unenjoyable. She realised the things she would miss and the loved ones she would hurt if she didn't make an effort to behave differently. Knowing that with the obsession gone she would have a huge void in her life we then went on to fill this new free time with pleasurable activities.

PHOBIAS

All our memories are coded in our minds. Unfortunately, we have a habit of accessing memories that are not good for us in preference to the ones that are. When a frightening experience is accessed repeatedly, all the negative thoughts and emotions associated with it get hard wired into our brains and a phobia develops. Ranging from anything from a fear of confined spaces to the fear of books, flowers and even laughter, phobias are many and varied. At the last count, there were over 500 of them and that's just the ones that have been documented!

Phobias can begin subconsciously, for example when a family member had a certain fear of something which was picked up when the sufferer was a child. Therefore, spiders might have become associated with an extreme reaction such as terror, screaming and creepiness. It's like growing up with someone who speaks a foreign language. Eventually you would learn to speak it too. Phobias can also start after a significant event, such as being bitten by a dog. As well as a fear of dogs the phobia may develop to an irrational fear of all animals that bite. This is because the next time the person sees a dog, a cat may be nearby. The sufferer's phobia program may then be updated to include cats.

One of the worst things about having a phobia is the limitations it imposes. It can affect what a person does in their daily life and put restrictions and demands on their family and friends. Not only do phobias often stop people venturing outside their house, but people with irrational fears can lose their confidence, their friends and their connections with their family. It is when all these issues become too much to bear that someone who is phobic will come to see us desperately wanting to be helped.

We'll say it again, PHOBIAS ARE NOT GENETICALLY INHERITED.

Everything we do is learned. So it can be UNLEARNED!

The phobia program can be detected and through effective psychotherapy it can be scrambled and fatally corrupted. What we will do is make sure that the messages that created the program are completely overridden by powerful new messages sent to the client's subconscious via their imagination. Because the human brain cannot distinguish between a vividly imagined experience and a real one, new response patterns can be installed. How often have you found yourself telling a story that you have exaggerated a little to make a bigger impact or to make people laugh, only to find that eventually you end up totally believing the exaggerated version yourself?

A major concern of ours is that people with phobias tend to seek out others with the same kind of fears so they can share their experiences to make themselves feel better. This can actually be counter-productive, because they often end up competing with each other to

126

see who is in the worst state. They also share details of how their phobia has affected them, which may inspire another sufferer to adopt new kinds of extreme behaviour. The continual influence of such messages via Internet "support" groups in particular, makes the problem even harder to deal with.

The other thing we have noticed is that long-standing phobias can become a kind of friend or safety net. That's because they usually satisfy three important human needs: "certainty," "significance" and "love and connection." There is security in the certainty of what lies ahead, the phobia gives them significance and importance and it provides them with love and connection to others in the same situation. In fact, some sufferers actually get very worried about being cured. They are concerned that they will suddenly lose their "identity" and lose the sympathy and attention they receive now.

So it is often the case that after curing someone of their phobia we will help them rediscover the person they really are by focusing on their accomplishments and determining the direction they want to go in. This kind of life coaching is extremely rewarding. Not only are we removing a negative mindset, but we are actually giving someone back their life!

"Men are not prisoners of fate, but only prisoners of their own minds."

Franklin D. Roosevelt

Creating new associations

When clients with phobias come to see us we identify where their phobia began and how it was created, what the fear means to them and how it is coded. For example, it may evoke certain images, smells, sounds and colours. Our job is to change everything about this memory so it is coded completely differently. To do this we may use Cinema Therapy and Visual Coding Displacement Therapy (and often both) which are based on the principal that people can be disassociated from a certain memory and have it scrambled up so it can't be accessed again. We also create very strong associations with things that elicit the opposite effect to that which the client is currently experiencing. For example, someone who imagines spiders as evil and creepy could associate them with looking like a cuddly little teddy bear with huge cute eyes and long eyelashes!

Alternatively, someone who formed a bad habit with alcohol or drugs of any kind can be re-educated to associate these substances with something that is repugnant to them. It sounds so simple, but if it is done with clarity and the suggestions are precisely timed, lifelong habits can be broken permanently in a matter of minutes. We also use these therapies to treat people with negative programming that triggers lack of confidence, panic attacks or smoking. Yes, to us even smoking is a ritualistic habit, NOT an addiction.

Changing the pleasure of smoking to nausea

When Mandy came to see us she had been smoking for 13 years and trying to give up for 10 of these. She had tried lots of different therapies, nicotine patches and plastic cigarettes, but was not successful with these approaches. Consciously, she knew that smoking was bad but unconsciously she was telling herself that she liked smoking and that it was associated with various rituals. For example, on her way to work she would light another one while waiting at the first red traffic light. Then she would have a cigarette with her morning coffee. She had programmed herself to include cigarettes at various points throughout the day.

Our job was to change the way her unconscious mind responded to the thought of smoking. To do this, we asked her to relax, close her eyes and think about the pleasure that smoking gave her. You could see her smile as the positive associations came into her mind. Next, we told her to think of something that she hated. She replied with, "fish paste." When it was suggested to her that she would be given a spoonful of fish paste to eat she started to retch as if she was going to be sick. At this point she was reminded to think about smoking once again. The thought of eating fish paste was also presented to her and repeated several times until she was about to wretch. We then continued to talk alternately about smoking then fish paste.

After this, we asked her what would happen if some of her cigarettes contained fish paste and she was actually smoking fish paste? Now Mandy thought about them tasting even worse than she had ever imagined before! When she opened her eyes we gave her a packet of cigarettes but she refused to take one saying, "Take them away, they smell like fish paste!" What we had done was create a very strong neuro-association between cigarettes and something that she hated and the two had now become inextricably linked.

The next day, Mandy told us that although subconsciously she didn't feel the need for a cigarette she thought that she would try one. She opened the packet and although the cigarettes smelled horrible she persevered and put one in her mouth and lit it. As soon as she had taken a couple of puffs she was violently sick. To this day Mandy is very much cured of her habit.

WATCH YOUR PHOBIAS AS MOVIES
If you don't like them, just record over them!

We tell the client to imagine they are sitting in a seat in the middle of a cinema looking at themselves in a small size black and white image in the middle of the big screen. (Being on the outside looking in and disassociating themselves makes it possible to deal with bad memories and not get so upset by them.) We then ask them to picture the scene as a still frame before their bad experience happened.

Next we tell them to imagine that they are leaving their body in the cinema seat and are floating into the projection booth. This double disassociation should take away all the feelings that are associated with the memory. (It is like hearing that your friend has been in an accident and you are shocked, but hearing that your friend's friend has had an accident is of no real concern as it's further away from you.)

Then we ask them to play the memory and to freeze the frame again at the end when they are safe. Now we guide them back into their memory by asking them to float into the screen, but as soon as they do instead of being black and white the picture immediately becomes full colour and the size of the whole cinema screen.

Finally, we tell them to run the whole sequence back-wards really fast, distorting things. So for example, if there is someone they don't like they give them goofy teeth and donkey ears and make them wear an orange ballerina's tutu and Wellington boots! They also add a silly soundtrack like fairground or cartoon music. By changing all the codings the memory has been scrambled. This means that the brain cannot play it back again. Now when the client is in a situation where that memory is usually accessed they will find that it isn't there any more. Their phobia program has been fatally corrupted FOREVER.

How this technique worked for us

When we first discovered this fantastic technique we worked with it constantly, testing out all sorts of situations and ridding ourselves of all our fears. As it is such a long time ago since we did all that stuff we can't really remember what phobias we had. However, that fact in itself should make you realise the power that you have when you use cinema therapy.

On the next page you will find a detailed step-by-step version of this exercise. To help you experience the full effect, you could record yourself reading the guidance (leaving long pauses between each sentence) and then listen to it back later with your eyes closed.

Relive the event from start to finish

Sit in a cinema

See yourself before the event

Float to the projection booth

Run the movie backwards

Step-by-step cinema therapy

This is a technique where you need to think quickly and clearly. Ensure you are sitting comfortably and there are no distractions. Have either a cuddly toy, your favourite music at the ready or a photo with a strong and positive memory at hand, something that makes you feel great. This will be your "safety anchor" should you need it, as you will be thinking about the last time you had a severe phobic reaction.

1. Think back to the event when your phobia began, or about most recent severe phobic reaction you had. Think about the event as if you are watching it through like a movie from the start. See yourself before, during and at the conclusion of the reaction and at the moment you felt safe once more. Mark out of 10 how scared you feel.

2. Now imagine you are sitting in a cinema. On the screen there is a black and white still picture of you just before you experienced the phobic response.

3. Imagine that you are floating out of your body and up to the projection room from where you can see the back of your head as you sit in the cinema looking at the black and white still picture of yourself on the cinema screen. See and feel the projectionist's glass window as you look down at the back of your head.

4. Make this black and white still image turn into a movie and watch yourself from just before the phobia experience all the way through until just after it ended. When you get to the time after the whole experience where you began to feel safe, stop the movie and freeze it. Imagine the moment as a still image.

5. Now see yourself floating out of the projection room, floating through yourself watching the movie and travelling into the still on the screen. Then immediately make the movie full colour and LARGE. Run the movie backwards as quickly as possible in a matter of seconds. You can also add funny music (*The Birdie Song* or any other ridiculous tune. The theme tune to *The Benny Hill Show* works a treat!).

Repeat this exercise three more times. Now mark out of 10 how you feel. If you still have any fear, repeat the exercise until the phobic response has gone for good.

Editing out the memories of a fun fair nightmare

Carla was a woman in her forties who suffered from severe panic attacks in social situations. Whenever she was around a lot of people, she could not relax, because of one particularly upsetting event in her past. She had been at a fairground late at night with her friend. They were the last two people to go on the big wheel, but when the ride came to an end the operator would not let them off. He left them suspended in mid-air while they both became more panic stricken. Eventually he did allow them to get off, but the two friends were now worried that they would be attacked. Screaming, crying and literally sick with terror they ran off. Although they managed to get away from the fairground, they were unable to escape their memories which had plagued them since that day.

Because the cinema was too public a place, we asked Carla to imagine she was at home watching herself on TV in scenes that happened before the dreadful event. She was asked to describe the way she viewed these images. For example, were they in colour? Was the picture small and distant or large and close up? She was then asked to imagine that she was standing in the corner of the room looking at herself while she was watching the TV from her favourite chair. Now though, everything about the images was the opposite. If the picture had been in colour now it was in black and white and so on. We also told her to imagine that the face of the man operating the fairground ride, a face that had haunted her for years, had turned into that of a pink elephant!

When she could imagine all this quite clearly, we told her to go up to that evil man and punch him in the nose. While she was back at the scene of her most revisited memory, we asked her to take her friend safely off the ride and to reassure her younger self that the whole event had no value in her life and that her future was going to be great. To complete this process of empowerment we told her to give her younger self a cuddle and to pull this relaxed and reassured version of herself inside her body.

At this point, we could see a change in her physiology. This happens so many times. It is as though a part of the person is left behind in the past. By pulling this missing part into themselves even long after the event, they are finally free to get on with their life.

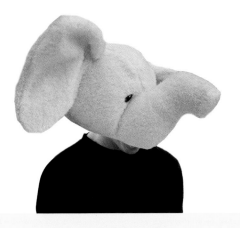

We scrambled the original codings and even the identity of the main character in this case, (making him look quite ridiculous) because the whole experience had been so deeply traumatic. Now, when that lady tries to replay that memory she feels nothing and social situations no longer scare her. In fact, now she no longer thinks of this memory at all.

VISUAL CODING DISPLACEMENT THERAPY

This is another versatile and highly effective treatment that we use extensively. Here, our client is asked to keep their head still and to follow the movement of an object with their eyes only, as it is moved in a circle in front of them. (The object we use most is one of Nik's watches). By doing this we can see which points of the circle evoke the strongest and weakest feelings associated with the phobia. At one point in the circle the fear will be greatest. This is because when there is an internal thought trigger, the person looks in a certain direction and accesses a particular part of their brain that makes them think about their phobia.

When their eyes flicker or their physiology changes, we know that we have struck upon the exact place they look when their fear is triggered. We ask for a calibration of this point, i.e., 10 out of 10. We then carry on looking for the point in the circle where they have either neutral or no feelings about the phobia. When we find this, we dilute the fear by moving the object in a fraction of a second from the point of fear to the point of no feelings. Whilst doing this we also make the client jump by shouting either "Whoosh!" or something related to the phobia, which helps break the pattern.

We then ask them to blink vigorously. Having carried out the dilution, blinking helps to refocus the eye and acts as a "reset" and a starting point. After repeating this process around five times we will once again calibrate the client to see where they are. Usually we would expect a reduction to 3 out of 10. Another set of five displacement processes would disperse the fear altogether.

have respect
for your
emotions

These days it's supposed to be cool to be impassive and not to react to any situation, good or bad. You see it all the time on TV and in the movies where actors show no emotions when faced with extreme adversity, as if they are somehow superhuman because nothing phases them. It's all about looking good and appearing invincible. In real life this is a very difficult and unwise act to try and follow. Our emotions are what make us human. They are also like a sixth sense, telling us when we need to take action, what decisions to make and what needs changing.

They are a vital part of us; they express the essence of who we are. Emotions are also an essential part of our intelligence. When we stop communicating emotionally we can become detached and socially isolated. Not to react with tears of joy when someone shows you kindness, unable to show anger, biting your lip so you won't cry and stifling your instinct to burst out laughing are precious missed opportunities to experience life at its most authentic. When we lose the ability to feel and to express how we feel, we are unable to make deep connections with others. Blocking or suppressing emotions can lead to loss of identity, loss of confidence and manifest itself as depression or other physical illnesses.

We see so many clients who have suppressed their true feelings for so long that they are scared of what would happen if they ever let them out. Would they make a fool of themselves? Would they ever be able to live with themselves again? Being fearful of people and everyday situations is very limiting and creates an imaginary prison that prevents us from being ourselves.

Fear (and its close relations anger, frustration, anxiety and hurt) can teach us an enormous amount about ourselves. When we experience painful emotions we can either ignore why they are happening and keep on endlessly experiencing them again, or we can stop, step outside the situation and look at ourselves, ditch our unfounded limiting beliefs and move forward... feeling much, much lighter yet stronger.

By looking at your own fear-based pain you will be better able to relate to the pain of others and form closer bonds. Life is not about acting cool to hide a fear of your emotions or people's reaction to them. Cool is a lonely place to be. People rarely regret being honest with themselves or expressing their true feelings. The time for regrets comes in old age when people look back and realise they weren't being themselves and nobody really knew them at all... not even themselves.

HOW WE HELPED KYM OVERCOME HER PANIC ATTACKS

When 30 year-old actress and singer Kym Ryder came to see us to help her overcome her panic attacks, we learnt that despite her young years she had experienced more than her fair share of personal hardships and was still carrying a huge amount of emotional baggage as a result. Our sessions with Kym involved several of the therapies mentioned in this chapter and are featured in our second series of A LIFE COACH LESS ORDINARY.

As an "inspiring life" Kym's is a classic rags to riches success story. At the age of 10 her father lost his joinery business. Consequently, the family was made homeless and was relocated to a local council housing estate and Kym joined a new school. Being a powerful singer as well as attractive and outgoing she became an obvious target for bullies who were jealous of her looks and talent. A group of older girls would hit her, take her money and shout that she was fat and ugly.

After leaving school, Kym sang in pubs and clubs and auditioned for theatrical roles. At 18 she became pregnant with her son David and went on to have a daughter Emily two years

"Yes, the Speakmans are certainly different. If there were more people like them, the world would be a better place."

Kym Ryder

later. She then split up with her boyfriend and life became quite a struggle financially. Home was a "fly-infested slum in Wigan" and Kym was too poor to buy her children a single toy.

When she was 24, her mother saw an ad for a TV reality show that was based on choosing members of a new pop band. She encouraged her go to the first auditions and although Kym never thought for one second that she would be chosen for stardom, that is exactly what happened. She shot to fame in 2001 as part of the group Hear'Say whose brilliant first single "Pure and Simple" sold 1.2 million copies and went straight to No. 1 (as did their album). A sell-out UK tour followed. "We played at Party in the Park in front of 100,000 people," Kym recalls, "When I look back on how much we did it's quite frightening."

Kym's rise to fame was all the more impressive not only because she was a single mother of two living on benefits, but because she had to battle against so many personal demons to realise her dreams. She pushed herself forwards despite the crippling self doubt and severe panic attacks that had plagued her life since her early 20s. But being an accomplished actress, of course she had been able to hide her fears magnificently! During her initial consultation with Nik and I, she described the attacks as being so severe she could not breathe. So she took more breaths in, would hyperventilate and felt as if she was going to die. She said it was one of the scariest things she had ever encountered. The attacks would strike at any time; when she was on stage or just sitting at home watching TV. Her doctor told her she was suffering from post-natal depression but she disagreed and refused medication. Despite numerous counselling sessions and hypnotherapy treatments nothing had helped her in the long term. Now the episodes had become so bad that they virtually ruled her life and were threatening her new career as an actress, which was one of the main reasons she had come to us for help.

Nik and I identified several reasons for the attacks. As we asked her about her fears, we discovered that she had witnessed a lot of illness around her as a child and as a result she had become conditioned to be terrified of death, including her own. Whenever she was ill she would imagine the worst and became consumed by the dreadful idea that people that she loved could die at any minute. The idea of cancer particularly terrified her.

So the first thing we had to tackle was her deep underlying fear of death. We also wanted to significantly reduce the uncomfortable feelings associated with her panic attacks. We used visual coding displacement therapy to find the trigger points for her anxieties and to dissipate intensely painful feelings by moving them to an area of her mind where there was little or no response. At one point Kym jumped quite noticeably as Nik moved the watch quickly away and asked her to blink.

Describing how she felt afterwards she said, "I feel like I have had a weight lifted off my shoulders and I feel lighter somehow." And in a newspaper interview later she revealed, "I felt like demons were leaping out of my body…" The therapy had effectively released a burden of deeply embedded toxic negativity from her subconscious mind.

We then progressed further with her to address her fear of driving. When we consulted with her we gleaned that she had developed this phobia as a result of a traumatic car crash when she was 15. We suspected that this might also have been another underlying trigger factor for her panic attacks. This time I took her through cinema therapy where she relived the experience but with less intense emotions. At the end, I asked her to remember the incident but she struggled to bring the images into her head as they had all been scrambled. In fact she said that she literally could not think about the event at all!

Another major event that was severely affecting Kym's life was the unexpected death of her granddad who had been her biggest fan and supporter. He had developed terminal cancer. But her parents had wanted to shield her from the pain so they did not tell her about his condition. Her granddad therefore died without Kym saying goodbye or telling him how much she loved him. This had now become a huge regret that was holding her back.

So Nik and I put on our lab coats and took Kym back to the past in our time travelling De Lorean. By taking her to a time in the past when her granddad was fit and healthy, asking her to recall all the good things that he had said to her and giving her the opportunity to say her farewells, Kym was no longer haunted by her regrets. Towards the end of this therapy, Nik asked Kym to give her granddad a big hug and told her that as she did so her arms would start moving inwards as he became smaller and gradually went inside her body.

When Kym got out of the car tears were pouring from her eyes... but they were tears of happiness because she knew that her granddad was with her and that she had finally been able to say goodbye to him properly. This was a very emotional moment for Nik too as he got to share such a special moment with Kym.

The final issue that we addressed with Kym was the bullying that she had endured as a child. Sadly, the insults had stuck in her mind ever since and were a major factor in triggering her panic attacks. From being a confident, extrovert child, the bullies had turned her into a shy, withdrawn shadow of herself who was full of self doubt. As an adult, Kym had learned to disguise her lack of confidence extremely well and few people suspected that she was actually fighting hard against a highly critical inner voice which was repeating the taunts of her bullies. Our Mental Shower therapy proved highly effective in washing away the dirt that had stuck to her all those years.

I asked Kym to close her eyes and think about the bad things the bullies had said. I told her that the insults had been soaked up into her subconscious just like written words on a piece of blotting paper. I asked Kym to imagine that all the nasty, hurtful comments had oozed out of her body and onto the surface of her skin. When I switched on the shower, I asked her to envisage all those horrible, untrue, unjustified and dirty comments being washed away and going down into the drain where they belonged with the bullies.

Finally, for some light relief, we ended the session ended with a paint fight, which was my way of showing Kym that she could now laugh at the girls who had made her life a misery.

We successfully released Kym from the dreaded prospect of having further panic attacks so she can now move forward with renewed, optimism confidence and freedom. She reportedly told her friends later, "I cannot believe it. I never thought I would shake off the condition."

Throughout the sessions Kym was totally open, emotionally sincere and fully accepting of everything that we asked her to do. Her attitude was fantastic and her honesty about her personal issues and the fact that she had bravely shared them on national television touched so many viewers. For weeks we were inundated with emails from people who identified with her circumstances.

Kym is a fantastic person who oozes resilience and tenacity and it was a great pleasure to work with her. Now all her negative ties have been cut she is free to move on and as Nik rightly said on camera, "We will see that Kym will have a fantastic future."

Since coming to see us Kym commenced a new role as barmaid Michelle in the country's most popular soap opera and we believe she is now a strong contender to win one of Britain's top Soap Awards (and rightly so!). We have also heard that she has been offered a mega deal to write her autobiography, which will certainly help and encourage the many people out there who face similar personal challenges. Kym is a fabulous and truly talented actress and singer who now has unlimited opportunities ahead of her. We look forward to seeing and hearing more of her on TV and seeing her inspirational life story in print!

"All my dreams have come true. I want to shout it all from the rooftops. I'm totally happy and my story could inspire others."

Kim Ryder

6.

Get the
happiness habit

"There is no such thing as **addiction;** there are only **bad habits** based on **bad thinking.** Change your **thinking** and you'll be **cured!!!**

Nik Speakman

The down side to so-called "happy pills"

When situations become too difficult to bear it is quite understandable for people seek help via counseling or mood suppressing drugs. Doctors normally prescribe this type of medication in much the same way as they prescribe a short course of antibiotics or any other drugs to help you overcome an illness. As life coaches, we are often asked to help people who have been voluntarily taking antidepressants many years after a traumatic event occurred. They want to stop but are fearful of the consequences. Will they lose their self control? Sink to rock bottom? Feel unbearably anxious all the time? These tablets become their imaginary armour so nothing can hurt them any more.

First of all, let's start by exploding a popular myth. Believe us when we say antidepressants do NOT make you happy! What they do is numb your emotions so you won't feel that bad. But you won't feel that good either. Actually you won't feel anything much at all. What people do when they take a "happy pill" every day is say to themselves, "I am depressed and I need these pills because I am unable to cope." Or "I am depressed and need these pills so I don't have to face what's making me sad." Then they tell themselves they will be on them for the rest of their life. No wonder they're miserable! Imagine going to bed with that thought in your head or waking up to it every day. In effect, people become practiced at being depressed, because it is somehow easier than making the effort to be positive.

We feel that the word "depressed" is thrown at people with little thought of its consequences. We have known clients who have visited their doctor following bereavement and they have been told they are depressed and given mind altering drugs and sent on their way with a new label. These people are NOT depressed they are grieving! What a wonderful world this would be if the word depressed was taken out of the dictionary. You would be "down" or "upset" or "out of sorts." Aren't these far better terms than DEPRESSED?

Another thing about antidepressants is that they are NOT addictive. What people actually feel towards their tablets is dependency. As you know, we believe there is no such thing as addiction, just a habit that has got out of control. Breaking a habit (or in this case, dependency) is all about belief. Think about your life before the traumatic event. However you were feeling then you can DEFINITELY feel that way again!

One lady who came to see us told us she felt her life wasn't worth living because she felt so lonely since her husband died three years ago. She was taking antidepressants and was like a zombie. After reminding her of her life before the pills, it eventually dawned on her that she had kept taking them long after they were needed in the belief that she was deeply depressed by nature. Realising she had stuck this label on herself for no good reason, she

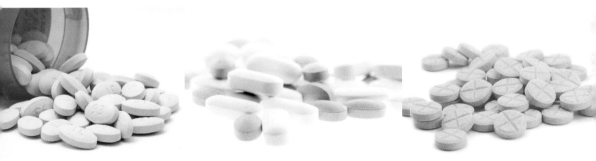

changed the perception of herself and having first consulted with her doctor, she decided to stop taking the pills. In fact, she was so determined to end her reliance on these drugs that we performed a little ceremony and danced around the toilet before she flushed them away! She came back to see us a couple of times afterwards because she was not used to feeling normal human emotions again. This lady had been completely numb before and thought her future was hopeless. She emailed us recently to tell us that, she is now far closer to the people she loves. Her life has changed from being grey, unfeeling and dull to being bright and full of sparkly smiles and genuinely happy, memorable moments!

Important: As with the above client, we do not advise anyone stops taking antidepressant medication without first consulting their doctor.

"the simplest way to a happy life is to smile!"

Eva Speakman

why you should
check out the **sky!**

We once heard of a therapist who specialised in treating people for what we consider that vile label "depression." The first step of his treatment was extremely novel as he would sit his patient down, ask them a little about their condition and calibrate their level of depression on a scale of 1 to 10. He would then break into their thoughts by asking whether they had noticed how many different types of chimney there were outside and proceed to describe several different styles himself. This no doubt left his patients wondering, "What's going on here? I came here for help, not to discuss the architecture of chimneys."

The therapist pressed the matter further by handing the patient a pen and paper and asking them to go outside and come back 20 minutes later having documented how many different types of chimney they had seen and making a sketch of the best one. This request must have appeared truly bizarre! However, and presumably hoping that the therapist knew what he was doing, they trotted out and duly completed their task.

Having studied the rooftops the patient would return with their sketch and information on the various chimneys. The therapist would then ask, "What did you discover?" As they described their findings, the therapist would break the patient's state again by saying, "Forget the chimneys, just tell me how you feel?" He would then re-calibrate the patient and discover, as he expected (and much to the patient's surprise) that there was a marked improvement in their level of depression. Marvelously some patients actually did not feel depressed at all! So what actually went on here?

How often do you notice the birds in the sky... the clouds floating by or even that the light

"𝔚hat guides us is children's response, their joy in learning to dance, to sing, to live together. It should be a guide to the whole world."

𝔜ehudi 𝔐enuhin

fitting on your ceiling is in need of a clean? Well the fact is, if you look up, you just cannot feel depressed easily. But if you notice people's posture and demeanor, you will see that most individuals look straight ahead at eye level, or more often downwards. Taking this into consideration, the odds of us feeling happy are not always favourable.

Furthermore, in most people's working environment they are sitting at a desk or counter so they will look down, just as I am doing typing this now. So could this be why children always seem so happy? Children have no option but to look up at the world! A recent study showed that children smile an average of 400 times a day, yet adults manage just 15. Children laugh approximately 150 times a day and adults only six. Children play for between four and six hours a day and adults do so for just 20 minutes or less.

We often tell people that they should rediscover their inner child, to take them back to experiencing life without complications and stress. When we are dancing around our garden beating a drum and shaking maracas with our kids the outside world thinks we are crazy, but the truth is... we are being children. Now we have another fantastic reason to become children so we can look up at the sky.

One final word of warning though. Although this is a fantastic tool for you to use, as we do as often as possible, please take care as we have had some very happy clients walking into lamp posts!

P.S. When I feel I can't possibly do another bicep curl, or when Eva is persevering with the last five minutes on the exercise bike, we have learned to fling our eyes up to the ceiling and "whoosh," that feel-good bout of energy washes over us and sees us through.

145

Inspiring lives...

Born in Washington in 1945, Hunter "Patch" Adams (he doesn't know where the nickname came from) was considered "a maths and science nerd" who got top grades with little effort. Sadly, his father died when he was in his early teens. Those years were very stressful and difficult for him and he was hospitalised twice with ulcers. Then he was devastated by the suicide of a beloved uncle. Patch considered killing himself too and overdosed on aspirin while standing at the edge of a cliff. His mother signed him into a mental hospital. After he was released he began phoning strangers at random, just to make human contact; something he says he still does today!

Having gained considerable experience of the medical world firsthand, Patch decided to train as a doctor and change the way healthcare was delivered. He hated what he thought medicine in the United States had become: a greedy, profit-focused impersonal industry. He believed that treatment should be provided *free* and that healing should be "a loving human interchange, not a business transaction." Good health, he observed, was more deeply related to close friendships, meaningful work, spirituality, wonder, curiosity, passion and hope. He recognised that these were time-consuming, impractical needs, but when they were not met, people become isolated, lonely and hopeless and were then diagnosed with depression or some other mental illness and treated with pills.

To provide a more humane approach to health care, Dr Adams set up the Gesundheit Institute ("gesundheit" means good health). In fact, 20 adults and their children moved into a large, six-bedroom house and called it a hospital. Supported by small donations and volunteer workers, the hospital treated people 24-hours a day, seven days a week. With medical situations ranging from birth to death, hundreds were helped every month, all completely free of charge. (Dr. Adams didn't want people to think they owed something; he wanted them to

"The most revolutionary act one can commit in our world is to be happy."

Dr "Patch" Adams

think they *belonged* to something.)

Initial patient interviews were three or four hours long as Dr Adams believed that only when deeper relationships were formed could great medicine take place. Drugs and medication were still given when needed, but large doses of reassurance and compassion was the standard prescription for all. With the philosophy that laughter, joy and creativity could help cure all ills, Dr Adams dressed as a clown to make patients laugh. A 6' 4" man wearing whacky suits in rainbow colours certainly drew attention. When he said, "I'm not a blend-in kind of guy," he was certainly not exaggerating.

Dr Adams soon needed a bigger and better hospital to meet the demands of his patients. As his ideas were too radical to get conventional funding he threw himself into campaigns to generate the five million dollars he needed to build "the first silly hospital in history." His vision was a 40-bed hospital complete with craft and exercise rooms, vegetable gardens and a theatre!

Thanks to his efforts to generate publicity, Hollywood producers soon learned about him and decided to make a film based on his life starring Robin Williams. The movie *Patch Adams* attracted much needed publicity for his cause. (It was through seeing the film that we first learned about the remarkable Hunter Adams and also decided what a fantastic name Hunter was, even though our son prefers Patch!)

Today, Dr Adams' treatment of patients mainly consists of emotional support, letter writing and entertaining. Working as a professional clown, performer, writer, movie maker and a public speaker, Dr Adams puts almost everything he earns towards his hospital project. When he is not fund-raising, he travels around the world to explore the possibilities of peace among nations and to entertain orphaned and hospitalised children.

Although Dr Adams is far from his target, he says he is not unhappy because the journey getting there is so fulfilling.

To make an online donation visit: www.patchadams.org Please help establish the world's first therapeutic centre for silliness. We love the idea!

> *"It does matter to your health to be happy. It may be the most important health factor in your life!"*
>
> Dr "Patch" Adams

147

why we all need a
healthy
sense of humour

Two researchers at the University of California have been studying the effects of laughter on the immune system. Their studies, which were published in the journal *Humor and Health* have shown that laughing is hugely beneficial to the human health. Just look at the incredible things a good belly laugh can do:

Laughing lowers blood pressure
Reduces stress hormone levels
Relaxes the muscles
Cleanses the lungs
Provides cardiac exercise (a bit like internal jogging!)
Boosts immunity to fight infection and increases the number of cancer fighting cells
Releases endorphins which reduce pain, aid the healing process and make us feel great!

All this is the absolute opposite of the way the body reacts to stress. These benefits are so powerful that they can even last until the following day. Plus there are absolutely no known adverse side effects (except hiccups!) What great stuff!!!!!

Laughter therapy: it's crazy but it works!

Laughter, even if you only pretend to laugh, is a very powerful antidepressant therapy. Sit with a smile on your face, put your shoulders back and try and feel lousy; you just can't do it! Studies have shown that people labelled "clinically depressed" can become extreme optimists just by laughing and exercising. Even forced laughter releases serotonin (a happy hormone) in the brain.

You may not be able to go through the whole day laughing, but you can SMILE even if it is just to yourself. Mother Teresa believed that "peace begins with a smile." A genuine smile puts us at ease, while permanently frowning will make us feel stressed and can even lead to illness.

Research by the French physiologist Dr Israel Waynbaum shows that the facial muscles that are used to express emotions trigger specific brain neurotransmitters. Smiling, just like laughing, releases healing hormones and immune boosting killer T-cells, whereas frowning triggers the secretion of stress hormones. Though a heartfelt smile has a deeper effect, even a surface smile will trick your the brain into releasing happy hormones! The more we smile, the more we will want to smile and the more it will encourage others to do the same thing too!

> "Most folks are about as happy as they make up their minds to be."
>
> Abraham Lincoln

> "If you're not using your smile, you're like a man with a million dollars in the bank and no cheque book."
>
> Les Giblin

How does laughter therapy work for us?

We use laughter therapy as often as we can. For example, we were about to embark on a 50 mile charity bike ride. Not only were we participating but we were supposed to be starting the race. We were all ready on time and raring to go... however we didn't plan for three flat tyres... and no puncture repair kits or spares! Did we cry? Did we lose hope? Did we decide not to bother? Did we stamp our feet in rage? NO, WE LAUGHED!

Through laughter therapy and a quick phone call to the event organiser asking for the donation of a puncture repair kit, we got the tyres fixed and although we set off 45 minutes late WE DID IT! We concluded the race, we didn't come last, we sang all the way and raised lots of money for a worthwhile charity!

Therapy to make you smile

★ ★

Try a smile trial for a minute. Relax your face and then smile slowly. Now frown. Can you feel the difference? It takes only 26 muscles to smile and 62 muscles to frown. So why put yourself under so much strain? SMILE. It's so much easier than *not* smiling.

Do a smile therapy experiment. Take note of how you're feeling and thinking when you are *not* smiling. Now think of a funny situation and SMILE. Notice how different you feel.

Make faces in the mirror! Every morning and evening stand in front of a mirror and with exaggerated mouth movements say, "Ha, ha, hee, hee, hoo, hoo" and hold the cheesiest of grins for a count of ten. Try it with other family members for maximum effect.

Shout "Morning World!" First thing in the morning before breakfast go outside, or put your head through the bedroom window and shout "Morning World!" Wave to the trees, the postbox, the birds and all your curious neighbours.

Give compliments. If you think something is nice, say it. Tell a stranger, the lady in the shop or another mum at the school gates… "I love your coat", "Your eyes are so sparkly," "Your laugh is infectious," "You've got a lovely smiley face" You will make their day and their positive energy will radiate back to you.

Have a happy night time routine. Go to bed applauding yourself for what you HAVE achieved, not what you didn't do.

Praise yourself. Look in the mirror, give yourself a smile and a hug and tell yourself "I AM FANTASTIC"

Every morning shout "MORNING WORLD… MORNING SKY… MORNING TREES…"

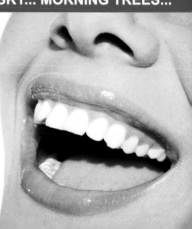

Whatever we are doing, we always try and add a bit of daftness to the day...and smiling is our top priority even if we've been up since 5.00 am! As you can see, we've been practicing the art of laughter therapy for quite some years now...

Make FUN a serious priority in your life...Practice a little silliness every day!

"A person without a sense of humour is like a wagon without springs. It's jolted by every pebble on the road."

Henry Ward Beecher

Create your own Circle of Radiance

1. Stand up and close your eyes.

2. Visualise or even physically place an imaginary circle in front of you. (The circle can be any size you like.) Give the circle a colour and add a soft humming sound to it if you wish, as if it was full of potential energy like Luke Skywalker's lightsaber in Star Wars!

3. Vividly recall a time when you were truly happy. See, hear and feel everything as accurately as possible. Savour the feeling... let it intensify... When you are positively oozing happiness, quickly step into the circle and squeeze your left wrist with your right hand (or vice versa if you are left handed). Continue to relive the feeling of total happiness as you hold your wrist.

4. Release the pressure from your wrist. Now imagine this amazing feeling of happiness dropping from your body and into your circle. (Some people see a sparkling energy zooming down into it.)

5. Step out of your circle.

6. Now repeat steps 3 to 5, this time recalling other empowering emotions and events. Think of a time when you were truly confident or a time when you felt invincible and very proud of yourself. You may have passed an exam, won an award, been applauded, received a fabulous gift, just given birth, been proposed to... anything that stands out as being an exceptional experience with wonderful memories.

7. As you channel each positive emotion into your circle you may see it changing colour, size or shape, getting bigger and brighter or more sparkly. The humming noise it made at the beginning might also be louder, the more positively energized the circle gets.

8. Now step out of your circle. Slowly reach down and carefully pick it up.

9. Imagine that you are squeezing your circle and compressing it down into a little ball.

10. Push your arm through the ball and wear it like an invisible bangle on the same wrist that you were previously squeezing. You can then access all those fantastic feelings by squeezing it again whenever you wish.

REMEMBER: As you go through life and experience more phenomenal events you must add these to your Circle of Radiance too.

We give our "Speakmanned" wrist bands to our clients as a permanent physical reminder of all the positive thoughts and memories that they experienced during their meeting with us. (Nik's is gold, and mine is clear and sparkly!) Some people use these wristbands as a tangible Circle of Radiance because every time they see it they are reminded of the great things about their life and of their many successful achievements. If they smile (either outwardly or to themselves) every time they see it that is a lot of smile therapy in one day!

Chris

"Thanks Nik, for the advice you gave me while I was helping to film one of your shows. We were just talking outside and you said some words that helped me lose two stone four pounds.

You were also treating someone on your show who had a problem with over eating and told them to make a Circle of Radiance to capture a time when they were happy with themselves. You advised that every time they felt the need to comfort eat they should step into the circle and stay in it until the feeling passed. I followed your steps to create my own circle and it works 99% of the time for me. And I wasn't even having the treatment!"

"The Circle of Radiance is amazing! If we are doing live seminars, talks, radio and TV interviews or anything that requires a huge surge of energy, passion and motivation, we whip out our bangle and soak ourselves in feelings of euphoria!

In my circle I have my wonderful wedding day and holding my gorgeous husband's hand. I also have the days my children were born and the day a client said 'Thank you for saving my life,' amongst many other phenomenal events!"

Eva Speakman

153

thanks...
for **everything!**

It's very easy to get drawn into the mundane aspects of every day life such as working to pay the bills, keeping the house tidy and making meals... When you can only think about a boring routine of any kind you may start being reactive and focusing on the drudgery of it all which will obviously bring you down. To guard against this mindset, Eva and I recall everything that makes us feel great and brings us joy; things that we might easily take for granted. As the saying goes, you only miss something when it has gone. Conversely, you can only really appreciate something if you take the time to acknowledge it. So every morning after shouting "Morning World!" we practice The Art of Gratitude.

This involves a little ritual where we focus on everything that enriches our lives and say it out loud. We start by being grateful for our own health, intelligence and ability to help others without question. We then extend that gratitude to each other and how blessed we are to be two halves that make one whole. Our gratitude spirals outwards to include thanks for our children and how fantastic they are and how we enjoy their laughter, health, sharp minds and unconditional love. Then we think about our wonderful friends and how they assist us in our quest to help others. Our appreciation extends to our pets, our lovely home, our beautiful cars and the fact we are free to choose what we want to do... Our gratitude list is enormous!

The purpose of this exercise is that it focuses the mind at the start of the day on how fortunate you are. You therefore start each day from a higher place if you should hit situations that try to drag you down. Problems will need to be pretty massive before they are able to make you feel bad. The great thing about this exercise is that it doesn't matter who you are, you can always find something in your life to be grateful for. Start with the smallest thing... hearing a bird sing, your child's smile or even the fact you had a good night's sleep! You can even be thankful for fears that never turned into reality, illnesses you never suffered or any other undesirable situation you have *not* experienced.

Academic studies have shown that people who describe themselves as feeling grateful tend to have more energy, optimism and feel less dissatisfied and more spiritually aware than the population as a whole. To illustrate this, two groups of equally happy college students were assessed. One group kept a weekly "gratitude journal. The group that kept a journal was healthier, exercised more and was more positive than the group that did not.

When you are really practiced at The Art of Gratitude you will eventually realise that there is something to appreciate in EVERYTHING that happens in life good and bad. Yes, even the worst situations, including death, poverty or sickness have an upside; you just have to shift your perspective. Remember, negativity is a weight that can pull you into a dark pit of

154

hopelessness. Negative thinking is a very easy habit to fall into and goes hand in hand with self pity. Both approaches only lead to a downwards spiral into nowhere. Instead of thinking "This is terrible... Why is this happening to me... It's all so unfair..." Look at what that bad situation makes you *appreciate*.

By accepting a situation you cannot change in an entirely different way, the burden of feeling aggrieved or worried is instantly avoided. This is because it is impossible to feel stressed or frustrated if you are practicing The Art of Gratitude as the two experiences are poles apart!

Finally, directly expressing gratitude is such a simple thing to do, yet it is something people often neglect because their focus is only on faults. For instance, instead of noticing all the things that annoy you about someone close to you, be THANKFUL for everything they do that helps makes your life easier, happier, better or more comfortable. A simple acknowledgment that someone is appreciated can turn a hostile relationship into a caring, close and peaceful one.

Gratitude dissolves negative feelings such as anger, jealousy, fear and defensiveness. For these reasons we absolutely recommend that you discover the hugely powerful effect of these two small, simple but amazing words: "Thank you."

> *"What if you gave someone a gift and they neglected to thank you for it, would you be likely to give them another? Life is the same way. In order to attract more of the blessings that life has to offer, you must truly appreciate what you already have."*
>
> Ralph Marston

The art of gratitude exercise

By practicing this exercise every morning as we exercise we are totally set up for the day and no matter what could possibly go wrong, it pales into significance as we are already so grateful for everything in our life that has already gone right so far.

1. Close your eyes and take a deep breath. Count to three and then release it. Now take three more deep breaths and release any tension or worries...

2. Let your mind drift towards thinking about all the people in your life that help, encourage, inspire, support and love you. Include parents, children, friends, teachers, work colleagues, role models... Say "thank you" to each one.

3. Now consider all your own talents, achievements, strengths and attributes, beginning each thought with "I appreciate my..." End with "I feel gratitude for being me."

4. Finally, let your mind run freely as you search out everything that makes you happy and enriches your life in some way... It could include anything from your pets and your home to your favourite pair of shoes or Ben and Jerry's chocolate fudge ice cream!

5. Now say out loud "THANK YOU FOR EVERYONE AND EVERYTHING I HAVE IN MY LIFE"

make a WOW! list

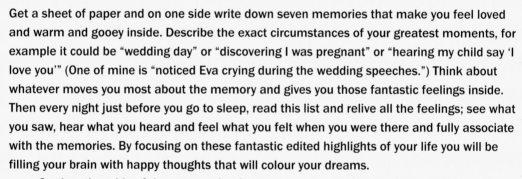

Many people have a tendency to beat themselves up over things that may or may not happen. They believe that they are somehow unworthy of happiness and do not deserve anything more than pain and suffering. This habitual mode of thinking will dictate the way someone experiences their future. If you make the decision to be unhappy then that is exactly what will happen because whatever you think will become your reality. If this does not sound like an appealing idea, it's time to change your mind about how you look at the world and how you view yourself. To shift your viewpoint, start by looking at all your WOW factors.

The edited highlights of your life

Get a sheet of paper and on one side write down seven memories that make you feel loved and warm and gooey inside. Describe the exact circumstances of your greatest moments, for example it could be "wedding day" or "discovering I was pregnant" or "hearing my child say 'I love you'" (One of mine is "noticed Eva crying during the wedding speeches.") Think about whatever moves you most about the memory and gives you those fantastic feelings inside. Then every night just before you go to sleep, read this list and relive all the feelings; see what you saw, hear what you heard and feel what you felt when you were there and fully associate with the memories. By focusing on these fantastic edited highlights of your life you will be filling your brain with happy thoughts that will colour your dreams.

On the other side of the paper write down seven aspects that you love about your life; things that make you feel amazing. Include at least three great things about yourself that made you feel proud, fired up, invincible or extremely happy. Once again, the key is to be specific. If passing your driving test was brilliant, concentrate on that memory. Which part made you feel proudest? Was it the moment you were told you had passed, was it seeing the examiner's face, or was it the moment you received your license? Focus on how you felt and the sights and sounds surrounding that feeling to recreate those emotions.

This time read this list in the morning. Relive all those feelings; see what you saw, hear what you heard and feel what you felt when you were there and fully associate with the memories and absorb those feelings. WOW! What a great start to the day!

How this exercise works for us

A WOW list is brief and to the point and makes such a huge difference. Our WOW lists are on laminated CD cover sized pieces of paper that are colour coded blue on one side for bedtime and yellow on the other for morning.

How could you not have a good night's sleep and be glad to wake up to a new day having reminded yourself of everything that is on it?

In 2001 we realised one of our dreams which was to swim with dolphins.

Eva's morning WOW List:

Nik, Olivia and Hunter
Losing 3½ stone in weight!
Olivia passing her school exams
Our TV series and radio work
Changing people's lives
Life!

Nik's morning WOW List:

Eva, Olivia and Hunter
My dad
Our TV series
Client emails and thank you's
Discovering that anything is possible
Life!

We got married twice in 1996: once in England and once in Florida because we have so many friends in both countries.

The birth of our first baby Olivia on Nik's birthday was an overwhelming day of emotion and celebration.

157

7.

The right terminology

"To be **Speakmanned** means you know exactly where you're going, with a big **smile** on your face, using the **right terminology** and it's like **'WORLD...I'M HERE!'"**

Eva Speakman

Say it, believe it DO IT!

Did you know that the unconscious mind cannot deal with negatives? So for example, if you tell yourself "I don't want to fail my driving test" your subconscious mind will interpret it as a positive thought and focus on the subject i.e. driving test. It will actually translate the command into "I must fail my driving test." Yes, believe it or not, this is what it does. And because it wants to do a good job of things, it actually encourages you to fail by conjuring up messages that fill you with self doubt and nerves. What you should tell yourself is "I am going to pass my driving test." Your subconscious gets the message loud and clear. It edits out the things that are going to stop you passing and gives you the very best chance of success.

This also works when you are talking to others. Is it any wonder that when you tell a child not to drop his ice cream this is the first thing he does? What you should say is, "Hold on to your ice cream." Think about what you are saying. If you use negatives all the time, that is how everything will turn out: negative.

Have you ever replied to the question "How are you?" with "Oh, I'm not bad." This assumes that your emotional benchmark is set at "bad." Your subconscious holds on to this thought and keeps pulling you back to this self imposed level. That's why we always say quite genuinely, that we feel fantastic! Put a big smile on your face, say the words and you are up there. So next time someone asks how you are reply, "I feel FANTASTIC" Whoosh... You're up there!

It is vital for you to speak to yourself ONLY in positives if you want to reach your goals. Instead of saying "I don't want to be unemployed" say "I want to get a job" instead of saying "I don't want to be fat" say "I am going to be slim." If you talk to yourself in the right way you will find that things start to go the way you want them to go as if by magic.

Talking ourselves out of success

Sometimes the reason we don't succeed is because we give up trying! And is it any wonder??? When coaching, or even just in social conversation, we hear so many people excuse themselves for giving up by using the fateful line, "But I tried everything." The fact is, if you had really tried *everything* you would have found a solution! If someone tells us this we would ask, "How many things did you try?" The usual response is, "Hundreds of things."

If this sounds familiar to you, go ahead and write a list of the hundreds of things you tried. We are quite confident you will start your list something like this: "Well, No.1, I did... No.2, I went...No.3, I called... errrm." Or maybe you just did the same thing over and over and guess what, you got the same result until you gave in. And thus concludes the effort!

STOP talking yourself out of trying! Keep adjusting, keep studying, keep trying and you WILL get there. The worst case scenario is that you would be honest and say, "I don't think it was for me after all!" Remember, it took many hundreds of attempts for Henry Ford to perfect the car and for Colonel Sanders to finally sell his chicken recipe and create the KFC empire aged 64!

Shift your vocabulary to
Speakman speak

Make negative words better by changing I'm feeling...

Annoyed to vexed
Anxious/stressed to a little concerned
Confused to curious
Depressed to a little out of sorts
Defeated to a little unsettled
Disgusted to surprised
Disappointed to ruffled
Embarrassed to aware
Exhausted to "I could do with a doze"
Fearful to curious
Frightened to curious
Frustrated to challenged
Horrified to a little surprised
Humiliated to uncomfortable
Idle/lazy to saving energy
Impatient to full of anticipation
Insecure to inquisitive
Insulted to misunderstood
Irritated to perplexed
Jealous to impressed
Lonely to having lots of time to myself
Lost to searching
Overwhelmed to in demand
Painful to uncomfortable
Rejected to overlooked/underappreciated
Scared to uncomfortable
Stressed to busy/blessed
Stupid to unresourceful/ I am learning
Not bad to could be better
Terrible to out of sorts

How to make **good words** # great!!!

Change I'm feeling...

Alright to FANTASTIC
Attractive to delicious
Awake to raring to go
Confident to unstoppable
Determined to on fire
Enthusiastic to excited
Excited to ecstatic
Fine to great
Fortunate to amazingly blessed
Fun to crazy
Glad to thrilled
Good to excellent/superb/dynamic/magic
Great to incredible
Happy to ecstatic
Interested to enthralled
Loving to passionate
Motivated to raring to go
Nice to fantastic/awesome
Okay to fantastic/brilliant
Perfect to awesome
Powerful to invincible
Pretty good to stunning
Satisfied to amazing
Secure to confident
Smart to genius
Stimulated to charged up
Strong to invincible
Terrific to FANTASTIC!

So consider this, "What would you do if you really knew that you couldn't fail?" When we ask this question most people say that they would do whatever they wanted. So why wait? After all ANYTHING IS POSSIBLE. If you have ever wanted something enough you have always found a way to achieve it. You know it's true because you already have examples of this in your life!

Three simple actions that speak volumes

1. Think Positively.
By thinking positively you are saying:
"I am an optimist."
"I am open minded."
"I believe it can be done."

2. Act Positively
By acting positively you are saying:
"I see adversity as an opportunity to learn or improve."

3. Speak positively
Speaking positively means:
"I am not a harsh critic or judge; you do not need to fear me."
"I admire and value my fellow human beings and praise good behaviour and success."
"I have the personal resources to help others."

labels are for
clothes not people!

Here's a little story that shows why labels are a really bad thing. A researcher took a class of students and randomly divided them into two groups. He then told one group's teacher that his students were really gifted and told the other teacher that his were slow learners. A year later, both groups had intelligence tests and the so-called gifted kids scored far higher than the "slow learners". Remember, both groups started off roughly the same in terms of ability.

In other words a label, whether it is applied by you or anyone else, can become a self-fulfilling prophesy. Labels we use to describe people include perfectionist, pessimist, addict, loser, bully, victim, racist, Catholic, Muslim... there are thousands more. The problem with labels is they can also become vehicles for negative assumptions. These assumptions will then create a reality that you believe is true.

When a label has no relationship to the person underneath it can be very hurtful. People who are shy are wrongly assumed to be snobbish, people who live alone are presumed to be antisocial and those with aspirations of a better standard of living are seen as shallow, smug or selfish. This is when labels turn into name calling and it's not just other people who do it. We do it to ourselves... and with far greater effect.

You may tell people you've always been unlucky in relationships, you've got no self control, you're an addict and you've got no self confidence. To make the situation worse, you may even seek out others who are in the same boat and compare and contrast the terrible things you have endured. (Yes, it is absolutely true, misery loves company!) At the end of your life, will you look back proudly and say, "I was the best alcoholic around." "There was nothing I didn't know about failure," or, "Nobody had a worse life than me."

It's very easy to get into a comfort zone and do what you've always done and get what you have always got. Then people moan about their lives and say I wish I had achieved this, I wish I had done something different. Anything is possible and it's what you *believe* that counts. Here are some myths that we want you to get rid of **RIGHT NOW**.

"A leopard never changes its spots"
"I was born like it/my problems are hereditary"
"Once a (insert label) always a (insert label)"

Everybody and we mean EVERYBODY has the potential to develop and grow. Human beings are complex and multidimensional. When we apply labels, we are prevented from seeing the fantastic, unique person underneath. Of all the 6.5 billion of us on the planet, NO ONE ELSE is quite like you.

You and your potential are totally UNIQUE.

Rid yourself of "always" and "never"

Black and white thinking is rigid and closes you off from so many possibilities. If you think that just because you have been divorced twice you are always going to fail at marriage and never meet the right person you might miss out on finding the perfect partner. By saying "I will NEVER be successful/rich/confident/slim…" "I will ALWAYS be a smoker/fat/shy/an addict/depressed…" you are fixing those labels even more firmly into your head with super glue. Listen to what you are saying to yourself. Can you hear those ridiculous generalisations? Do you think you are being fair to yourself? NO. WE DON'T EITHER.

> "All that we are is the result of what we have thought."
>
> Buddha

> "Your own words are the bricks and mortar of the dreams you want to realize. Your words are the greatest power you have. The words you choose and their use establish the life you experience."
>
> Croquette Sonia

eliminate
 ## inhibitions and hesitation

 Hesitation and inhibitions can stop us from being able to let go and be truly happy. The best way to change any habits is to quite literally delete those programs from your brain as you would delete them from a computer. To do this, you can literally shock them out of your nervous system! We have read of many ways of how to overcome hesitation and our favourite is still so wild and wacky that we just love it. And of course like all the other exercises it works amazingly well. So what do you do?

 First you need to identify the areas in your life where you feel anxiety, hesitation or have inhibitions of some sort. You then need to visit a commercial premises such as a petrol station, shop, bank or fast food outlet, preferably when it is busy and make a totally absurd request such as asking for something that they don't sell or don't do. Please remember to be pleasant and non-threatening. When they have explained that they do not do or sell what you want, just thank them and leave politely. Repeat this a few times during the same week at different premises.

 You will notice that future situations where you would have felt anxiety and hesitation that you will feel totally different and you will become liberated! A lot of our coaching patients do tend to express concern regarding what the person behind the counter may think or do. So let us reassure you that in all the feedback that we have had with this exercise, the response has been usually shock and confusion followed by amusement. The key is to maintain your composure, be polite and look confused when they say "no." If anyone reading this is now thinking this exercise is foolish or pointless then, sorry, this exercise is exactly what you need, and you should do it for two weeks.

Hi, can you tell where I can find the centre of the universe please.

...and a return ticket to Never Never Land.

Two special meals and an extra large life jacket please.

Do you have any lead balloons?

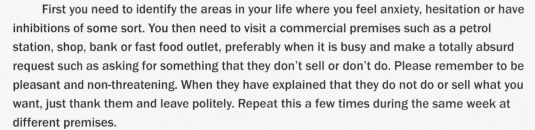
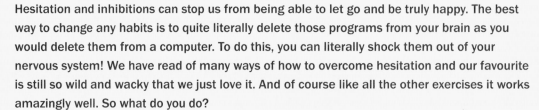

I'm looking for a pink panther... do you have any in stock?

So how does it work? Basically, we have all been conditioned by our environment against making mistakes in public; therefore we feel total embarrassment when we do. As our nervous system then becomes set to protect us against this uncomfortable feeling, we hesitate before speaking as we don't want to make a fool of ourselves. However making mistakes is an important part of growing up. Yet the older we get the more worried we become!

Remember when you fell off your bike when you were a kid? You just got straight back on without any issues? What happens when you get older is that the first thing you do is look around to see if anyone saw you! Even if you are hurt, the physical pain is nothing compared with the possible feeling of embarrassment.

Our favourite way of doing this exercise (we still do it about once a year just to exorcise those "embarrassment demons") is to walk into a major fast food outlet with a huge queue and wait in line holding a pair of shoes. (Incidentally, while waiting in line you will feel the tension build, even though you are in no danger. Your adrenalin starts pumping and your heart will start pounding. This is just the neurology of your conditioning and nothing more.) When it is our turn to be served, we smile at the server and with a totally straight face say, "Please can you put new heels on these shoes for me?" The look you will receive is amazing and you will usually get, "'WHAT?" We then reply, "This is a cobblers isn't it?" When you are told, "No!" you say, "Thanks anyway" and walk out. Awesome!

The server then usually discusses you with the next person in line and if you say it loud enough, there will be several people behind you thinking that you have just lost it. The good news is, that is exactly what you *have* done. You have begun to lose the anxiety, hesitation and inhibitions that were holding you back.

NO!!?! What was that you said again?

Very funny dear

Sorry, what was that?

NO - sorry we don't!

A complete nutter

167

MORE WORDS FROM THE SUCCESSFULLY SPEAKMANNED!

Ellie

Before I met the Speakmans I felt like I had lost my sense of proportion when dealing with problems. I was extremely stressed because of the pressures of taking on a new job. I had also been taking antidepressants for a year, restarted smoking (after quitting for 7 years) and I had started to bite my nails.

After my consultation I felt a great sense of relief. Nik and Eva understood my feelings and their outlook on life made perfect sense to me. We discussed the side effects of antidepressants and they gave me the confidence to stop taking them. (Actually, I had not seen any positive effects from them in the first place and had become lethargic and somewhat detached from my emotions.

I stopped taking them and felt peculiar as the drugs were washed out of my system. But by our next meeting I felt a massive change in my outlook and general well being. I had also stopped smoking and biting my nails because I wanted to prove I had control over my urges. I found the technique of asking myself questions to establish the root of my problems very effective.

Another revelation was that my outlook on life had become particularly negative and I needed to change my language and interpretation of events. For example, I took derogatory comments personally. But I found them easier to deal with when I understood why people belittle others. I also realised that people can behave differently when they are striving to feel significant. I started to take a step back and consider situations before they became overwhelming. I often felt like a computer that needed "de-fragmenting" and after talking to the Speakmans all my files would go back into their rightful place and I would feel a surge of optimism.

I still experience surges of panic when I feel I have no control over a situation but I am getting better at interpreting events more rationally. I have now learnt that I must "dance with the devil" in order to gain control of things. I have made some major improvements although I am still a long way from where I want to be. But I know I will get there in the end thanks to the Speakmans and everything they have taught me.

Andy

In the past six weeks I have managed to lose one stone in weight, I have done this by being careful with what I eat and I have also been doing a lot of RKD (that stands for Rapid Kitchen Dancing). I also recently discovered that a close friend of mine has had some serious money troubles. Boy did they need help. They told me they were behind on the mortgage and were going to have their home repossessed.

In the last month I have sorted all of their debts out with them by making phone calls, writing letters, talking to experts even more importantly teaching them how to save and plan ahead. All of their debts are now clear and their mortgage has only gone up by £50 per month. Can you believe they could have lost their home?

The reason I am mentioning all of this is because when they thanked me they said, "How are you so positive and so focused?" I have to admit never once did I let them think that we couldn't succeed in turning the situation around. All of this is because of the Speakmans. They restored my faith in human beings and in myself. Their zest for life triggered a fresh start for me. If they hadn't helped me, I couldn't have helped my friends and their six year-old son, who could all have been out of their home by Christmas.

Paul

I now look into the future with my mother standing there waiting for me to show her what I'm up to. WOW! The people who matter to me are now there instead of my past. This may seem bizarre, but when I step in to the future I now do so with 360 degree view and not the old two-dimensional view. Thanks to the "dream catchers" I'm free to catch mine and that makes me feel fantastic!

Lily

As an actor you are faced with insecurity and if you don't have a support mechanism in place at home, life could get quite daunting. This is what happened to me, I wasn't succeeding as an actor as quickly as I would have liked. I wasn't focused enough and had negative days. Nik and Eva gave me the confidence and self belief which has helped me to move on and achieve my goals. I now have faith in my ability to succeed as an actor and I will. I want the organisers of the Golden Globe awards to put my award aside as I'm coming to collect it!

(Lily has now moved to Hollywood and is auditioning for movie and TV roles.)

10 Speakman golden rules

2
SET GOALS!
If you don't define exactly what you want in life, how will you know if you are heading in the right direction? It's like trying to get to your destination without a map.

1
STRETCH YOUR IMAGINATION!
Success is not limited by your place o birth or the color of your skin, it is only limited by the size of your belief. Make yours ENORMOUS!

3
SET DEADLINES
Reaching goals takes time. Set realistic dates and work towards them.

4
PUT IN EASY MILESTONES
Don't try and change everything at once. Break your goals down into a series of steps. Success is the sum of small efforts that are repeated day in and day out.

5
EMULATE SUCCESS
Success leaves clues. Whatever you want, find someone who already has it and use them as your guide.

170

6

BE FLEXIBLE

If what you're trying to do isn't working stop, think and learn from the experience and move on to a better way of getting there. You don't make mistakes, you just find new ways of doing things. Every adversity will bring you a benefit of some kind.

7

MOVE OUT OF YOUR COMFORT ZONE

Successful people make a habit of doing things they don't want to do. You will get the furthest when you are willing to do and dare. The "sure thing" boat never gets far from shore.

8

BE PERSISTENT!

Persistence will overshadow anything - even talent!

9

SURROUND YOURSELF WITH POSITIVITY!

The more exhilarating your friends and your career, the more flowing and fulfilling your relationships and pursuits will be.

10

CHOOSE HAPPINESS!

Happiness is not a result, it's a choice. Ditto misery and hopelessness. Stop blaming and complaining. Remember, if you want more love, give more love. If you want more peace, give more peace. If you want more happiness, give more happiness.

"We are not embarrassed about our success. Clients come to us because they want to be more successful. If they didn't know that we were successful ourselves then why should they accept our advice?"

Nik Speakman

8.

Welcome to our world

we don't
just talk about the **good life**
we live it!

In our TV series A LIFE COACH LESS ORDINARY we opened the doors to our home and our lives not to brag or to impress, but to share and inspire. We are proud of what we have achieved and see it as proof that anyone can make their lives whatever they want them to be, wherever they started and despite the inevitable potholes along the way. (Yes, even *our* lives have not always run smoothly as you will be able to discover through our forthcoming joint autobiography!)

As life coaches whose clientele includes the rich and famous, we have helped media celebrities and sports stars to identify what is holding them back and have shown them how they can achieve more in their professional and personal lives. In our mission to change as many people as possible we also treat people of all ages and occupations from lawyers to stay-at-home mums.

Our policy has always been to guide by example. You would not seek advice about giving up smoking from someone with a 40-a-day habit, or take golf lessons from a novice. So why on earth should you accept life coaching advice from anyone who has not been successful in their own life?

If you gauge success in terms of spiritual fulfillment, our hearts are filled daily with the warmth of those we have helped to reclaim their lives. If you measure it by material rewards, we have got everything we ever dreamed of and live in a home that in our opinion is literally fit for a king. If you measure it in terms of personal happiness, we're not just on cloud nine we're on cloud nine million! And if you measure it in terms of personal progress we haven't just gone that extra mile, we've gone to infinity and beyond!!!

Stubley Hall

Our Magnificent Centre for the Soul

We have always loved Stubley Hall, so when it went up for sale in the year 2000 we immediately arranged a viewing. We actually had no intention of moving from our lovely stone farmhouse overlooking Hollingworth lake, but we felt ourselves somehow being drawn to the place. It was a gut feeling, something instinctive and almost spiritual. We just had to have it!

We made an appointment on the Friday, viewed it on Sunday, made an offer on Monday, entered a contract race on Tuesday and exchanged on Wednesday! At this time, we hadn't even put our house on the market but we just wanted it so much. This is the essence of what we do. To be able to grow, you've got to push yourself to the next level and trust your instincts,

or as we would say, your subconscious.

Originally a family home built in 1277, Stubley Hall was a restaurant and wedding reception venue before we bought it. We decided to restore it to its former Tudor manor house glory but as it is a Grade 2* listed building, this took a bit longer than we thought. While we were waiting for our planning applications to be approved we moved into a drab three-bedroom flat on the premises, which reeked of tobacco and dogs. Little did we know that it would be almost five years before we would be granted planning permission.

Despite this setback we kept our vision. Our conversion now consists of an elegant tiled hall featuring a contemporary cloakroom. We have transformed the former bar area into a comfortable, spacious lounge that is just breathtaking with its huge stone Tudor fireplace and mullioned windows. Our dining room was once the Great Hall and above it there's an impressive galleried landing with the most incredible original oak beamed ceiling with wind braces. The kitchen, the heart of the house, is the most amazing and awesome kitchen anyone could wish to have. We designed it ourselves and it's just very, very "us."

Upstairs, our master bedroom suite has its own limestone wet room and huge open stone fireplace with a remote control fire! It also features the most spectacular original 16th century stained glass windows; it is truly fantastic. Although things did not go exactly to plan with the time it took to obtain planning permission or even after that when we had started the renovations, we kept focused on our outcome: the end

result, and did everything within our power to make it happen. Things kept going wrong so we adjusted our approach and when things went wrong again guess what, we adjusted our approach again and again until we got it right. There were many points where we could have said, "Oh no, what have we done?" sold up and moved into something more manageable. But we stayed passionate and tackled each challenge as it came along. As Shakespeare said, "Nothing is good or bad, it's only thought that makes it so."

We consider our home to be a gift to share, and everyone who comes to visit will find that there is no work/home divide. Wherever there is a place that we feel would be appropriate for someone's treatment we will use it, whether it's the gallery for Magic Mirror therapy, the garden, where we perform Box and Burn ceremonies or even the ensuite bathroom where we use Shower Therapy to wash away bad memories. And of course in the grounds there is Nik's garage complex which houses his collection of fabulous cars, including the famous De Lorean which we use for our unique Back to the Future therapy.

Visitors are often quite touched that we are willing to open up our living space in this way. So for those who have never been inside, here is a short guided tour of our home and an insight into the wonders of Speakman World!

Clockwise from top r/h corner: The grounds of Stubley Hall with characterful stone statues. Bottom row: Our Tudor-style knot garden, fun 'fake' sheep, personally named street and historic mullioned windows. Left: Eva in the kitchen of our dreams! Top: The Old Hall with original 13th century wood beams.

Top: Old drawings that show Stubley Hall as it was in its original Medieval form and later with 16th century additions.

Above: Our ghost Fatima, whose portrait now hangs above the fireplace in the family room.

Stubley Hall is home to a few friendly ghosts too!

During the time we have lived here Nik and I have experienced what can only be described as "strange happenings." For example, we have had a clock moved and our ice cubes freeze upwards in spikes! It is thought, and this is not necessarily our belief but something we have been told by a psychic healer, that as well as our human body we also have a body made of vibrating energy which survives physical death and retains consciousness. At the time of physical death this "duplicate spirit body" goes into an energy sphere that can accommodate those vibrations. The theory is that ghosts are energy that have not completed this journey because of some unresolved emotional state or they are just happier in a certain place or building. Apparently, the longer they stay behind the harder it is for them to find their way to the spirit world, which might explain why one lady is allegedly still with us.

Legend has it that the house is haunted by a beautiful woman in white called Fatima, who would often play the harp for Ralph De Stobbeley to whom she was engaged. When he was called to fight in the Holy Crusades in the 13th century, he gave Fatima a jewel encrusted crucifix and promised that when he returned they would be married. Later, on hearing that he had been captured, Fatima cut her hair short, dressed as a cabin boy and boarded a ship to help rescue her beloved Ralph. Regrettably the ship was struck by the plague and Fatima died before finding her true love.

Eventually Ralph was released and returned to Stubley Hall to find that his family's wealth had diminished. He consequently agreed to marry a wealthy French princess. The wedding took place at the Hall on Christmas Eve. That evening, Ralph heard the sound of a harp playing in the woods and went out to see who was making such lovely music. Ralph did not return. The following morning, his new wife and family sent a search party out to look for him and found him dead with the look of shock on his face. They also noticed that Ralph was clutching something in his hand. When they prized his fingers open he was holding the jewel encrusted crucifix he had given Fatima.

According to legend, if you stand in the grounds on Christmas Eve you can hear the sound of a harp playing and you may even see Fatima's ghost which still haunts the Hall today. When Stubley Hall was a wedding reception venue it is documented that she would target new brides by tripping them, ruffling their hair or tugging on their headdresses and jewellery because she was jealous of their happiness.

Fatima is not the only entity who lives with us. We have been told that four other ghosts have not moved on. There is a woman in a yellow dress named Zelda and three children: Elizabeth, Felix and Jonathon. Being curious to find out more about them, we invited a team of psychic investigators round. They believe that human minds are energy stations which create, transmit and receive energy. Therefore thoughts, (which are waves of energy), can be transmitted to and from human minds and other living people and entities in the afterlife.

One of the team, who stated that he had telepathic powers, apparently made contact with a seven year-old boy called Jonathon who told the investigator that we hadn't lost our childhood and that he loved us. This was heart warming to hear. The investigator also told us that the gallery was one of the liveliest, happiest places he had ever visited and that we had created an environment so vibrant and energy-packed that the ghosts were feeding off it. What a fantastic compliment. Being able to energize the living and the dead!

These photographs really surprised us. An orb appears across my chest in the photo at the top. And if you look closely at the trampoline above just to the right of my feet, there is a ball of light, which also appears to be an orb. Orbs are believed to be a ghost's energy or soul in the form of balls of light. It thought that ghosts find it easier to manifest themselves as a ball of light because it takes less energy. However, when the weather gets colder and there is more static electricity in the atmosphere they find it easier to take on shapes other than orbs. It is also believed that they are able to draw on other energy sources when needed. All we know is that positive energy attracts more positive energy and our house is crammed full of the stuff whether there are such things as ghosts or not.

yellow lamborghinis
and plenty of
bling
these are a few of
our favourite things!!!

Everyone should accumulate wealth responsibly and be proud of how they have earned it. There is a huge difference between setting out to make money at any price (usually at the expense of others) and attracting money to you by offering the world the very best of yourself that you have to offer.

We are so proud of what we have achieved and everything we spend our money on reminds us of those achievements. Our cars, our clothes, our vacations and all the objects in our home are symbolic of everything positive that we have accomplished as people.

There are rewards for being the best at what we do. Nothing we have or anything we own has been obtained for the purposes of trying to impress anyone. We love and appreciate nice things and the fantastic side effect of having these material things is that we can impress upon people that they too can have whatever they desire. In brief, IF WE CAN DO IT SO CAN YOU!

Many of the most precious things that we own are actually gifts that we have received from our clients. Every time we look at them we feel uplifted and recharged because they were given to us with so much love and thankfulness.

The Lamborghinis are not bought to impress; they are something that we are both passionate about. They remind Nik of the huge goals he set himself as a teenager and of all the obstacles he has overcome to reach them. Their ability to drive and motivate, inspire and energize is worth more than any monetary value. They add an extra brilliant dimension to life and driving them feels GREAT!

Anticlockwise from the top left: Our Lamborghini Diablo SV in Monte Carlo, Eva and I with our Lamborghini Diablo SV, Harley Davison VRSCA and Ferrari 355GTS, Eva with our Lamborghini Gallardo Spyder, our Ferrari 550 Barchetta, Plymouth Prowler, our black Humvee and our pewter and yellow Hummer H2s.

"Clothes are never a **frivolity** they always mean something."

James Laver

"Your **appearance** illustrates to others **how you expect to be treated.**"

Ellen Peterson

"We've got a **great image** and we **feel good** about ourselves and that **rubs off** on other people."

Nik Speakman

WHY THERAPY IS IN FASHION

We love attractively designed clothes that are not stuffy and conventional but reflect who we are: eternally young, fun, and zingy! We try to buy the best because it makes us feel good. It's as simple as that! Even if we had less to spend we would still prefer to invest in one great item rather than lots of discounted goods. You will never regret buying one fantastic piece that makes you feel really special. A closet full of "buy one get one frees" will eventually be discarded with as much ease as it took to acquire them in the first place. So if you have the choice, invest in better quality items; just buy fewer of them and go shopping less often.

Surrounding yourself with attractive things is also very therapeutic. It is uplifting to walk into a room that has been wonderfully designed and thoughtfully decorated. A view of a beautiful garden through a window, a sea that is lit with the colours of a sunset, even an attractively presented plate of food can make you feel wonderful. If you use money to create a beautiful environment you are making your life fantastic in more ways than one. Apart from the obvious monetary value that it adds to your home, you are bringing calm and tranquility into your life. It has already been proven that patients who have beautiful views or look at beautiful things experience shorter hospital stays and benefit from quicker recoveries.

Wanting to be surrounded by the finer things in life is not trivial or self indulgent. We are all instinctively attracted to that which makes us feel better. So listen to your instincts, ignore the hype and ignore the so-called fashion rules. If you try something on and it makes you look and feel amazing, buy it!

The problems start when buying things becomes the ONLY thing that gives you a boost, or you buy things when you can't afford to.

Items that are meaningful to us include (from left to right): our display of precious wedding memorabilia, porcelain cups which were sent to us by a friend, and a soothing floating flower display in our kitchen.

spend
positively!

We treat many shopaholics whose uncontrolled spending and the debt that goes with it is really just the tip of the iceberg. The real reasons for their problems are associated with negative self beliefs and distorted ideas about the meaning of possessions. Shopping can turn into a form of bingeing: something to fill an empty hole in a person's life. Once the cause has been identified, breaking a serious spending habit is relatively straightforward.

When you only spend to impress or intimidate, all you are doing is creating yourself a glorified prison to shut out the rest of the world. And when you use money to "buy" acceptance, approval or gratitude you are saying that whatever you have to offer as a person is worth less than the gifts you have purchased. (It is also pointless, because nobody wants to think their emotions or opinions can be bought in this way.)

Giving can take many forms, such as a smile, a hug, a thank you, or just a kind word. It is often this kind of gesture that is most appreciated and memorable. Also, the biggest gift that you can give a child is TIME. No amount of toys and presents will ever be so precious or more wanted that your undivided attention. So spend *time* with your children: read a book, play games with them or take them to the park. Many parents buy their kids new things to make up for the fact that they have ignored them. Children soon learn to see through this guilt trip and will push for all kinds of things based on your feelings that you "owe" them. Remember, all you really owe them is love and attention.

It is important to recognise what money is, and how it can work best for you. As with your role models (choose carefully!) you should be careful what you wish for. You do not want your life to become cluttered with expensive mistakes that you quickly begin to regret. Wealth should be a blessing not a burden.

When you go shopping, have a clear idea about what you are looking for. Take your time. Think before you buy and make it a golden rule when you are clothes shopping NEVER to buy the first thing that fits in the first store you visit! Ask the assistant to put the item aside for a few hours. Shop around and try on different outfits. Then, if you still haven't found anything better, buy it.

Remember the lessons you learned from decluttering your house. Every item you got rid of once came into your house in a nice shiny package or wrapped in tissue paper like a precious gift! There is a fine line between the things you buy today and the things that you will probably throw away... Think about how your new purchase will fit into your life. Will you REALLY use that bread making machine or use that expensive purple designer bag with diamante motifs and gold metallic buckles more than once? Is it worth it? Or will it cost you far more in terms of guilt and regret in the longer term?

They say that money talks. So tell the world about your success personally, thoughtfully and in your own unique and meaningful way. Look at every item you ever bought and ask yourself if it really reflects who you are and consider whether it makes you feel happy. Get rid of anything that is associated with bad memories or anything that makes you feel drab. Surround yourself with meaningful possessions that are worth more to you than their price tag. By spending with your heart and only buying what truly inspires you or benefits others, you can turn your money into an enormous positive force for the good!

These are traditional dragons that were given to us as a gift by a client who we had cured of a long-standing phobia. They guard the house from evil spirits. We love them!

9.
How to be fantastically energized!

"Man can not live by bread alone…he needs Swamp Joose too."

Nik Speakman

"People say to us, 'All you eat is green stuff and all you drink is that green juice, how boring!' I say to them, 'We have so much more time to enjoy life. It's like we're plugged into the socket and getting loads of energy!'"

Eva Speakman

turbocharge
your
energy levels

When Nik and I got together we didn't have a healthy lifestyle at all. Everything centred around rich food and alcohol or crisps and chocolate. We kind of expanded and started slowing down, which made the problem even worse. Then there was a realisation that we were getting fat and unhealthy. So we set ourselves a new goal, just as we had done with our businesses. Our target was, "LET'S GET FIT."

Once we looked into it, we discovered that different foods can completely change the quality of your life. Some have a draining effect, others make your feel *AMAZING*.

Since he started bodybuilding in 1977, Nik has experimented with different diets. In fact, we have both discovered so much about healthy living over the years that we would love to share our joint knowledge with you right now. But as this isn't a healthy lifestyle book we will save that for another day. However, we do want to share with you the basics to get you started. It is no use if you are totally focused, you have a positive mind and physiology and you are using positive terminology but you have no energy! Read on and you will find out how to discover the "Speakman energy dynamo" that you may have kept suppressed for so long.

If two former fat couch potatoes can do it...

Being firm believers that you should practice what you preach, here is an insight into the choices we have made. Look at the effect they have had on our health and life and ask yourself, "Do I want that?" If the answer is "YES," then we would be humbled for you to use us as your role models. Think of it this way. We have road tested everything that's out there and narrowed it all down to the absolute BEST choices you can make if you want to look and feel

Nik and I certainly used to like a drink!

GREAT! We are talking a full natural body lift here!!!

Look how eating energizing food has changed our appearance and our lives. If you think we are lucky and blessed with great bodies we will let you in on a secret, we weren't! What we do is based on the simple idea that if you eat bad stuff it shows on the outside and also where it really counts, on the *inside*.

When we set ourselves the goal of achieving total fitness we did it very specifically. We also made up our minds that this was a lifestyle change that would take time to develop and become an established routine. We were not looking for overnight weight loss, but long term vitality that would sustain us for the rest of our lives. Nik and I visualised the outcome and worked to make our visions a reality. We imagined ourselves being able to run round effortlessly, having tons more energy and looking slim, healthy and toned. We thought about the way we would like to look, the clothes we'd like to wear and most importantly how we wanted to feel.

Then we did our research. We discovered that the average Western diet with bread, meat, dairy, pasta, sugar, alcohol and caffeine was making our bodies far too acidic and making us sluggish and overweight. So we cut them out! GONE!!! Did we miss them? Yes, but we had some tricks up our sleeve which we will tell you about later.

Next, we looked at the nutrients that our body's organs needed to function properly and what they needed to help it get rid of toxic by-products. This is where we made some really radical changes, including the introduction of our miracle blend drink Swamp Joose® that we drink several times every day. This, plus our 10-Point Energy Plan is the basis of the magical formula that literally keeps us going!

SPEAKMAN SWAMP JOOSE®
Power packed with gazillions of nutrients

We think of Swamp Joose® as our nitrous oxide. It gives us our "whoosh" and get up and go! Our amazing formula not only hydrates the body, it gives it a good flush out and energizes every single cell. Made from an array of grasses including wheatgrass, spirulina, B vitamins and amino acids it is also very alkalizing and thus helps to balance the body's own pH.

What we eat and why we eat it

YES, we do eat real food too! BUT there are things that we know will make our cells stay healthy and things we know that will age us and make us feel drained. The following pages contain a summary of what we have learned over many years. Read it and think about it. If you only follow one or two recommendations we GUARANTEE you will feel better than you do today. At the very least start by drinking more water. Just do it! It will give you an instant pick-me-up, just like a wilting plant that is revived by rain after a drought. Honestly, you will wonder why you thought you could live like a camel before!

stop the
rust
to avoid disease

Why do we put oil in a car engine? Quite obviously to make it run efficiently, smoothly, make it last as long as possible and protect it against wear. So what would happen if you started pouring acid in your car oil? I am sure you would know what to expect, which is why no one in their right mind would ever do that. Yet this is something most of us unknowingly do to our body's engine oil, our blood, every single day.

Our bodies are generally more alkaline, so pumping acid into your body and therefore your bloodstream is just like putting acid into your car engine. The scary fact is that in just the same way, the acid will make you corrode and rust from the inside out. This corrosion is known as cancer and disease! To stop the acid corrosion you body has to produce cholesterol to coat your arteries. Of course, if you're putting acid in your body's engine you will soon begin to slow down. You might feel sluggish, bloated, tired and lethargic or suffer from headaches, arthritis, indigestion or a combination of all of them.

Human blood pH should be slightly on the alkaline, scale between 7.35 and 7.45. If the blood pH moves below 6.5 cells stop functioning and the body starts to die. So what are the acids that are making you rot from the inside out? The main and most corrosive acid forming elements are SUGAR, FIZZY DRINKS, VINEGAR, ALCOHOL, COFFEE, INACTIVITY and STRESS.

So when you get out of bed in the morning, late for an important meeting, drink a strong black cup of coffee with two spoonfuls of sugar and then drive off to work you will have unwittingly started the day on a huge overdose of acid.

Stress on all levels, whether it is physical, emotional or mental causes the body to overproduce acid wastes and upsets our delicate alkaline/acid balance. When blood becomes too acidic, the body goes into overdrive trying to maintain the right pH level by drawing on its reserves of alkaline minerals such as sodium, potassium and magnesium, which can eventually lead to chronic disease. Once your calcium stores are depleted, it will pull calcium from the bones and teeth to neutralise the acid. This then contributes to bone loss or osteoporosis. Cancer cells too prefer highly acidic environments, however, the good news is that cancer cells do not do well in healthy, alkaline environments.

When you eat sugar you also weaken your body's immune system. The over-acidification of the body ferments sugars, proteins and fats as opposed to simulating them for energy. When the body is in this state of fermentation, just like a battery corroding, once its alkaline energy has been drained, the body's natural cleansing process slows down and becomes a fertile breeding ground for disease and bacteria such as yeast, fungus and mould! These bacteria then excrete their own toxic waste into our blood making it even more acidic. This leads to low energy, poor digestion, constipation, diarrhoea, allergies and inconsistent bowel movements. You may also experience body aches and discomforts that just don't seem to disappear. Does any of this sound familiar?

Just take a look at a brand new battery; it is shiny and clean. But once the energy has gone if you leave it over a long period it begins to corrode, leak and go rusty. Have you ever found an old torch only to discover that when it didn't work it wasn't just that the batteries had been spent, but that they had leaked and rusted the connections? Or has this happened to you with a watch battery or something similar? Most people can relate to this experience. As you do, just think of yourself as a battery. The acid/alkaline balance is perfectly illustrated using this metaphor. When it is new, a battery is alkaline; it is full of energy and strength. Once the energy has been drained, all that remains within the battery is acid, resulting in leakage, rust and corrosion. This is exactly what will happen to you if you do not take steps to become more alkaline by reducing your acid intake and increasing your alkaline intake.

So now think of yourself as a more expensive rechargeable battery. To recharge, you will need to eat alkaline food which will make you feel healthier, fitter and livelier and will keep

"High energy is a must! The most amazing life in the world can seem mediocre if you don't have the energy to enjoy it."

Nik Speakman

ALKALINE-INDUCING FOODS: SWAMPJOOSE, ASPARAGUS, ONIONS, PARSLEY, LENTILS, SEEDS, SPINACH, BROCCOLI, GARLIC, CABBAGE, CUCUMBER, PEPPERS, TOMATOES, AUBERGINE, CAULIFLOWER, PUMPKIN, SPROUTS, GREEN BEANS, CELERY, CARROTS, BEETROOT, KALE, MUSHROOMS, RADISHES, LETTUCE, PEAS, SEAWEED, GINGER, CHILLI PEPPERS, SWEET POTATOES, WATERCRES

your energy levels sky high just like the brand new energy filled alkaline battery.

The correct ratio of acid and alkaline forming foods is difficult to determine because the balance is altered by chewing, food preparation, lifestyle, genetics, exercise, blood type and mental outlook. But in general, an alkalizing diet is one in which at least 70% of our food intake comes from alkaline-inducing foods which help to reduce the acidity of the blood and other tissue fluids in our body. If you are prone to infections, viruses, excess mucus problems and other toxic acidic conditions you may need to increase the alkaline content of your diet even further.

So what *is* an alkaline food? Basically GREENS and LOTS OF THEM, such as broccoli, celery, cucumber and spinach. Or you can get a high strength dose by drinking freeze-dried grass formulas like wheat grass or our very own Swampjoose.® Other highly alkalizing foods include asparagus, onions, parsley, lentils, seeds, garlic, lemons (after they are metabolised they have an alkalizing effect), watermelon, limes, grapefruit, almonds, cold pressed olive oil and some herbal teas like dandelion and nettle.

The other 30% of our food intake can come from acid-producing foods like cereals, dairy, eggs and meat. However, as has been mentioned before, very acid-forming foods such as refined sugars, canned soft drinks, caffeine and alcohol are best cut out altogether. Don't worry, we'll help you find something good to replace them with!

...APPLES, TANGERINES, PEACHES, PINEAPPLE, RAISINS, CHERRIES, AVOCADO, LEMON, LIME, PEARS, RHUBARB, BLACKBERRIES, COCONUT, DATES, GRAPES, MELON, PAPAYA, APRICOTS, BANANAS, STRAWBERRIES, RAISINS, ORANGES, NECTARINES, FIGS, PLUM ALMONDS, CHESTNUTS, TOFU, WHEY PROTEIN, CINNAMON, BEE POLLEN, MINERAL WATER, MOLASSES, FRESH FRUIT JUICE, BERRI

Alkalized equals energized!

Start the day by drinking a half a litre of warm water (not hot) with freshly squeezed lemon juice in it. Breakfast is very important. As it says, it is your break-fast (the break of your fast) so eat a breakfast cereal that will not raise your blood sugar too high such as All Bran or preferably an oat and millet mix with prunes. Prunes are fabulous because they contain more than double the antioxidants of blueberries and three times more than spinach, so you'll be off to a great start. Try swapping cow's milk with soy or almond milk and see what effect that has too.

Substitute dairy with more green vegetables or almonds, pumpkin and sesame seeds which are better sources of calcium. No living thing continues to drink milk after weaning except human beings. So think about where the cow gets its calcium. Yes, it eats green grass! Why not follow their example and drink at least one serving of green grass formula every day. One glass contains 11 times more calcium than milk!

Stop drinking coffee! YES, GIVE IT UP NOW. If you drink black tea, add a bit of skimmed milk to it so the calcium in your stomach is not absorbed by the tannin in the tea. Instead, drink herbal teas, water, tomato juice, carrot juice or low sugar fresh fruit juices (not from concentrate). Better still, invest in a juicer; it will inspire you to make all kinds of brilliant nutrient-rich original blends.

But if you do buy them, make sure you choose juices that are *not* made from concentrates as this basically means that the original fruit juice has been boiled down to condense it, which kills all the natural vitamins. This is why the manufacturers usually proudly state "with added vitamins" as if they giving you a big bonus. When you start getting the health buzz you'll be reading all the labels too, just like we do!

Eggs have long been known as "perfect nutrition in a shell" because the egg white contains all of the amino acids necessary for proper human nutrition and digestion. However eggs are not recommended for anyone who is dairy intolerant. Whenever possible, choose organic eggs because they are produced without the use of antibiotics, growth hormones or pesticides. Always wash the egg shells before you use them... just think about where they came from!

Drink lots of water all day long. Water helps your body get rid of toxins and assists various digestion processes. Food cravings are often the body's way of crying out for water. Drink more of it and you could end up losing weight without even trying! Many people ask us how much water they should drink. It is documented that you should drink at least eight glasses of water a day. While this might be okay for me, as Nik is double my weight it is not okay for him. To keep your organs hydrated so they work properly the recommended formula is 0.6 fluid ounces of water per pound of body weight per day.

If you are blood group O, you can eat red meat up to six times a week. However, if you know your blood group and you happen to be blood group A, all meats are best avoided as they will induce an unfavourable chemical reaction. Meat and blood group A are NOT compatible, as you will learn in the following pages. Eating red meat and sugar can fuel cancer cells, so the worst possible combination is barbequed red meat marinated in a sauce containing sugar.

Cut back on bread. Bread contains gluten, which is a sort of glue. So if you must eat it, choose the whole grain version and only have 2 to 3 slices a day. Alternatively, try the wheat-free alternatives such as rye crackers, rice cakes, pumpernickel or rye bread. Also, an enormous percentage of the population is wheat and/or dairy intolerant without realising it. If you suffer with IBS, bloating, headaches, wind, irregular bowel movements, constipation or diarrhoea, this could be the culprit. To find out if this is you, cut out dairy and wheat products for one month each and notice how you feel when you introduce them back in again.

Our 10-point energy plan

1. We alkalize to energize!!! To flush out the corroding acids we drink lots of water, nettle or dandelion tea and our Swamp Joose® formula.

2. We eat lots of living food (not stuff that's dead or has been incinerated in the oven or deep fat fryer). This means raw or fresh steamed veggies such as broccoli, celery, squash, spinach, red peppers and cucumber. To me, shopping for veggies with the wonderful choice that's available is *almost* better than buying shoes!

3. We take a Milk Thistle supplement to support our liver, which is our "well-being warrior."

4. Avocado is "God's butter." We use it like butter on toast, in mash or in a jacket potato for a creamy and healthy alternative. (For amazing garlic toast rub a garlic clove over a piece of hot toast, "butter" with avocado and sprinkle with oregano... YUM!)

5. We avoid coffee and alcohol like the plague.

6. We have cut out bread and pasta but occasionally eat spelt or wheat-free pasta.

7. Beans and brown rice are our main source of carbs.

8. We never eat pork or animal fats.

9. We avoid full fat milk, cheese and other dairy products.

10. We cheat once a week. (We like to indulge in French fries, buttered toast, chocolate biscuits and pink champagne!) If you eat healthily all the time then your metabolism slows down. A cheat day makes your body think, "Oh, I have to go to work now," and it revs up trying to process all the junk food you have eaten which keeps the metabolism running at a good pace.

Making sure we alkalize to energize in conjunction with eating the correct foods for our blood group makes us feel FANTASTIC!!!

If you ABSOLUTELY crave something so badly that your life would be miserable without it then substitute as follows:

French fries - Use cooking spray to coat thickly cut potatoes (or better still, sweet potatoes) and oven bake instead.

Try grainy mustard or avocado on a baked potato for a low-cal alternative to butter.

Potato chips - Kettle chips are much lower in saturated fat. Or make your own parsnip or sweet potato crisps the same way as the French fries, except sliced very finely.

Chocolate - Make a low-cal chocolate drink made with half the recommended amount of water. Allow to cool and blend with banana. Partially freeze, beat with a fork and refreeze for a great ice cream consistency.

Cheese - Reduce its fat content by gently melting in the microwave until the fat separates away. Pat the cheese with a kitchen paper then put in the fridge to cool.

Sponge cakes - Substitute half the amount of fat with natural yogurt, fat-free or light cream cheese, light or fat-free sour cream, apple sauce or prune puree when baking.

Cookies - Substitute with rice cakes or low cal muesli/granola or fig bars.

198

The emotional
freedom technique

Here's a little trick to help you beat any cravings, whether it's for coffee, cigarettes or anything else you are unhealthily attached to. The Emotional Freedom Technique (EFT) is a form of acupressure based on the energy meridians used in traditional acupuncture. But instead of using needles you tap key points on your face with your fingertips while you talk positively to yourself. This combination of tapping and positive affirmation will restore the balance of your body's energy system and help turn feelings of desperation into disinterest.

Some years ago Eva was a chocolate addict. Chocolate bars, cakes, biscuits, ice cream, drinks... ALL chocolate. EFT stopped her from bingeing on chocolate long enough to get it out of her system and realise that there *is* life after chocolate!

STEP 1: Think about your craving for a particular food.
STEP 2: Rate your desperation to eat it on a scale of 0 to 10.
STEP 3: Tap the underside of your left hand (the part you would use to do a Karate chop) against your open right hand while stating your craving. Then talk to yourself positively saying, "Even though I crave... (whatever it is) I am a unique human being and I love and accept myself." Repeat your affirmation three times.
STEP 4: Using your index finger and middle finger, tap on the top of your head and the facial points shown opposite 8 to 10 times each. Complete the sequence by tapping your sides, (halfway down your ribcage) and then finally, the inside of both wrists 8 to 10 times each. Be firm, but not so hard that you hurt yourself! As you tap on each point in sequence, remind yourself why you are doing this by saying, "My craving for... (whatever it is)." As you tap gently, receptors under your skin will transmit signals to your brain, just like you would tap your keyboard to send a signal to your computer.

When you have completed the tapping, rate your craving again on a scale of 0 to 10. If your craving has not completely disappeared, repeat the process.

1 - Inside eyebrow. 2 - Side of eye. 3 - Under the eye. 4 - Under nose. 5 - Under mouth.

199

different vehicles need different fuel

So often people think that because they look okay on the outside they must be okay on the inside. Believe us, looking okay is not the same as feeling FANTASTICALLY ENERGIZED on the inside. The best description we can use for being energized is that we feel bright, alert, positive, on top of the world and we just feel lighter. It's so hard to be precise about how you will feel, but we know that you'll know when you get there. Once you have felt the difference you will never be happy with just "okay" or "not bad" ever again. You will also look amazing: slimmer, with brighter eyes, shinier hair and that expensive health spa glow.

One of the main things that stops us feeling our absolute best is our choice of food. Yes, you have heard it all before, sugar, caffeine, alcohol and trans fats are no-nos. But this still leaves you with a lot of other food options, some of which might not be quite right for you. Since we discovered this system, we have experienced a massive boost in our overall well being and general health. Eliminating foods that stressed our immune system and introducing those that help to maintain its balance takes us back to the car analogy. If the manual says that you need to fill up with unleaded petrol but you decide to use leaded, you will seriously damage your engine!

Every time you eat, a chemical reaction takes place between your blood and the food you have consumed. The way your body reacts is genetically inherited and is caused by proteins in foods called lectins. 95% of these lectins are disposed of by the immune system, but at least 5% enter the bloodstream. If these proteins are incompatible with your blood type they will target an organ or bodily system and begin to lump together with blood cells in that

"The best seven doctors in the world are sunshine, water, rest and air, exercise, diet and love."

Eva Speakman

area, causing all kinds of health problems. To start with though, you will just feel sluggish and tired which is the starting point for disease.

So the first thing you need to do is find out what your blood group is. If you are not sure, ask your doctor to look it up on your medical records. Then you can start to adjust your eating habits accordingly.

A blood type way of eating works in harmony with your cellular profile. Each food group is divided into three categories: **HIGHLY BENEFICIAL** (food that acts like medicine), **ALLOWED** (foods that do no harm and provide nutrients, vitamins and minerals) and **AVOID** (foods that do not promote health). However, 75 to 80% compliance works well for most people so you can have "forbidden" foods occasionally if you wish.

Eating foods that are compatible with your blood type can help you lose weight and will restore the body's natural genetic rhythm to achieve health and vitality by increasing your resistance against allergies and infections, by helping you overcome stress and by delaying the ageing process. Try it for a few weeks and experience how great it makes you feel!

Here are the most beneficial foods according to each blood group type. Exceptions to these are listed under AVOID. Try and choose organic, chemical-free products wherever possible. Generally speaking, if a type of vegetable, fruit, fish, cereal product, meat or dairy product is not specifically listed it will usually fall into the "allowed" category.

> "It is health that is real wealth and not pieces of gold and silver."
>
> Mahatma Gandhi

> "For he who has health has hope; and he who has hope has everything."
>
> Owen Arthur

These photos were taken by Olivia on a 2006 holiday to Egypt where we were experiencing one of our life goals which was to visit the Pyramids and ride on a camel!

Blood Type O

Type Os tend to have a high stomach acid content which means they can metabolise meat easily but dairy products and grains are not beneficial and the gluten found in wheat can cause weight gain. This group also has a tendency towards low levels of thyroid hormones which can lead to metabolic problems.

HIGHLY BENEFICIAL: Red meat, lamb or cow's liver, fish, vegetables and fruit.

AVOID: Cabbage, Brussels sprouts, cauliflower, mustard greens (which inhibit the production of thyroid hormone) bacon, ham, pork, pickled herring, smoked salmon, corn oil, cashew nuts, peanuts, kidney beans, wheat flour, potatoes, melon, coconut, vinegar, corn syrup, pickles, mayonnaise, coffee, distilled spirits and black tea. Dairy products and eggs should be restricted.

Blood Type A

Because this group is predisposed to heart disease, cancer, and diabetes it flourishes on a vegetarian diet. Type As also have low stomach acid content which means they have a hard time digesting meat.

HIGHLY BENEFICIAL: Vegetables, tofu, most seafood, grains, beans, fruit and cold pressed olive oil.

AVOID: Meat, all dairy products (except yoghurt, mozzarella, Feta, goat's cheese, goat's milk and ricotta) anchovies, haddock, halibut, mussels, scallops, shrimps, prawns, corn oil, brazil nuts, cashew nuts, kidney beans, wheat-based products, mushrooms, vinegar and mayonnaise.

Blood Type B

If you are lucky enough to belong to this group you should be able to avoid severe disease and live a long and healthy life if you eat properly. Fortunately, you have a head start because you are inherently resistant to heart disease and cancer! Type B is the only blood type that can fully enjoy a variety of dairy foods, although wheat is not tolerated very well.

HIGHLY BENEFICIAL: Dairy, lamb, cod, mackerel, grains, beans, oats, rice vegetables and fruit.

AVOID: Chicken, pork, shellfish, cashew nuts, peanuts, wheat-based products, blue cheese, couscous, lentils, artichokes, tomatoes, corn, coconuts, star fruit, pumpkin, corn syrup, cornstarch, ketchup and distilled spirits.

Blood Type AB

Chicken contains lectin that will irritate the blood and digestive tracts of Type ABs. However, dairy foods are tolerated fairly well. This group should eat plenty of the vegetables and alkaline-producing fruits as they do best when their muscles are slightly alkaline.

HIGHLY BENEFICIAL: Seafood, dairy, lamb, turkey, tofu, beans, legumes, grains, vegetables and fruits.

AVOID: Beef, chicken, shellfish, Brie, Camembert and Parmesan cheeses, whole milk, corn-based products, artichokes, bell peppers, pasta, coconut, oranges, cornstarch, corn syrup, vinegar, distilled spirits, sodas and black tea.

fat
is our **friend**
make it yours too!

We are commonly told that when we are trying to lose body fat that we should avoid fats in our diet as opposed to including them. This results in people trying to eat less fat so they can continue to eat more varieties of specially manufactured diet products. In essence, they become vulnerable to marketing campaigns offering the fantastic benefits of fat free and low fat foods. While these marketed foods may be low in fat they are almost always high in sugar which can promote massive releases of insulin. This can have far worse implications for your health. Furthermore, the message makes us think that eating fat will make us fat and too much fat is a health risk. NOT SO!

Everyone has heard about the link between too much dietary fat and the risk of heart disease due to high levels of cholesterol. We often see TV advertisements warning us of the dangers of foods containing cholesterol. So is it any wonder that so many people fear to eat fat as they automatically believe all fat indicates raised cholesterol levels.

Cholesterol incidentally, is what our body **produces to coat and** protect its cells against acid foods like sugar! **The truth is that eating** some of the correct fats is essential to all human life. All **our body's cells** are coated with biolipid, which is a fatty layer **that protects and** maintains the integrity of each individual cell.

Without dietary fat we cannot absorb vit**amins such as A, D, E, K** and calcium, which in itself is detrimental to **our health. And let's face it,** meals with fat taste better and therefore the **chances are you will be** more satisfied after a meal and actually end up *eating less*. **Through** experience you will know that the combination **of low fat and high sugar** foods can leave you feeling hungry, dissatisfie**d and craving sugary or** starchy foods like chocolate and crisps.

YES... some fats should be definitely be **avoided. In particular,** animal fats and man-made trans fatty acids, **also known as trans fats.**

As a rule, trans fats are usually found in anything that has to sit on a supermarket shelf for a long time, like baked goods or products in jars. If you look on a food label, trans fats are sometimes listed under the guise of partially hydrogenated oils. Unlike natural fats which will promote you to use fat as an energy source, trans fats do the opposite. They make you store fat and use sugar as an energy source. A diet that is very heavy on trans fats or hydrogenated fats may ultimately contribute to diabetes and heart disease.

So, which are the best fats out there to stop you storing fat and how can you use them? The simplest way to do this is for you to consider there are two types of fat: saturated and unsaturated fats. Unsaturated fats consist of polyunsaturated fats and monounsaturated fats. It is the monounsaturated fats that are the good guys and the ones we should consume on a regular basis. The main sources of these are avocados, linseed oil, olive oil, fish oils, beans and some nuts like almonds.

Most experts would agree these are the best types of fat available as they contain fatty acids called Omega 3 or Omega 9, which provide protection against a wide range of diseases as diverse as cancer, diabetes, respiratory diseases, schizophrenia and gingivitis. Also, a moderate amount of these fats in our daily diet will prevent the body from storing fat and assist in the absorption of fat-soluable vitamins.

Aim to have your meals mainly comprising of vegetables, and choose foods rich in Omega 3 and 9 fatty acids. Drink plenty of water, herbal teas and add some exercise... even if it's a wiggle while you walk! Vastly reduce or eliminate your intake of sugar, cut out caffeine, alcohol, pastries, cakes and anything with a crust.

By following theses tips, you can help train your body to burn fat instead of sugar which will give you a fantastic and unlimited energy supply. Studies tell us that from the approximate 150,000 calories stored in the human body for energy, only 2, 500 of those will come from sugar. A further 23,000 calories are stored from protein whereas 124,500 calories are available from FAT. That is almost an endless supply of energy!

Comparing our body to an engine, everyone is aware that without oil the engine seizes and burns out. The same concept is true of the human body. So please, please DON'T BE AFRAID OF FATS. We have made them our friend and we'd like you to make them yours.

Finally, next time you see something labelled LOW FAT, just say "OK... hello sugar!"

TRIED PILLS...STILL FAT...TRIED THE HIGH PROTEIN DIET...STILL FAT...

FORGET DIETING AND DIET PILLS FOREVER!

If you have tried to lose weight you may have been tempted to try some of the "magic" slimming pills that are available today, mainly through the post. You know the kind we mean: "Lose up to 6 lbs a week in your sleep" "The latest amazing fat burning formula" "Miracle herbal blend shifts fat fast" If you have been persuaded to part with cash for these dieting tricks then you will already know that they don't work. But to save anyone else from falling into the same trap, we think we should tell you a bit more about these so-called answers to a prayer.

Most of these pills contain laxatives which produce short term weight loss. So when you stop taking them, obviously the weight will go right back on again and you will probably suffer from constipation. Some pills also contain ingredients that expand to fill your stomach or diuretics which encourage your body to lose water which could harm your kidneys. Do you really want to risk having all these problems to temporarily lose a few pounds? The only slimming pills that really work are available ONLY on prescription. There's a reason for this: they contain amphetamines ("speed") and are extremely addictive. Fatigue, depression, anxiety, sleeplessness and menstrual cycle disorders are the common side effects of regular use. These drugs are just not worth it.

Special "no this no that" diets

If you cut out various foods from your diet you should do it because of a good reason. If you are intolerant to wheat or dairy or certain foods are not chemically in tune with your blood group, then by all means stop eating them and see if you feel better for it. But to cut out ALL carbohydrates or ALL fats simply to lose weight will not make your body happy at all. If your body isn't happy, you won't be either.

We have already explained why you need the right kind of fat in your diet. Without

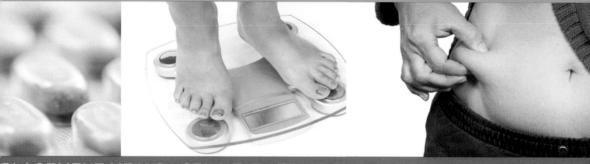

PLACEMENT MEALS...STILL FAT...TRIED THE CABBAGE DIET...STILL FAT.

Omega 3 and Omega 6 oils your hair will become dry and dull, your skin will start to shrivel, but more seriously, you will become vitamin deficient in A and D. These soluble vitamins are needed for healthy brain function. So cutting out fat altogether could literally make you start losing your mind!

Then the opposite to this is to ONLY eat fat and protein and cut out carbohydrates. The first thing that will happen is you will develop diarrhoea. Long term though, it is doubtful you will feel better as the body NEEDS carbohydrates to function properly. Without them, you will become tired, dizzy and irritable. High protein diets are also potentially dangerous as they put the kidneys under too much pressure. So if you have a kidney disorder you could be in serious trouble.

The best diet should be one that you look forward to eating every day. So all you have to do is make sure that whatever is in your fridge or cupboards is right for your blood type, fresh, natural, nutritious and absolutely DELICIOUS! And if it's cooked, it should be home made so you know what is in it. This way you will get a double benefit: weight loss and a fantastic feeling of health and vitality. It will be a feeling that you have probably never experienced before. Once you get there you won't ever want to go back to being a tired, despondent, flabby, confused, scale-obsessed weight watcher ever again...

Eating is natural and it should be a joy. Never force yourself to be thin by starving or taking pills. You need to think long term and use food to help you maintain a healthy weight and feel great now and FOREVER!

Here are five thoughts to repeat daily and put into your subconscious mind:

1. I will only have delicious fresh and natural food in my kitchen and NO JUNK!
2. I will listen to my appetite and tune in to what my body needs when it needs it.
3. I am only going to eat when I am hungry and STOP EATING when I feel full.
4. I deserve to feel and look fantastic!
5. I am a unique and special human being and I love and respect myself.

Recipes from the Speakmans' kitchen

Heavenly Hummus

400g (14 oz) canned chickpeas
(also called garbanzo beans) rinsed and drained
2 cloves of garlic crushed
Half a medium sized avocado
1 heaped tbsp cottage cheese

1 tsp olive oil
Squeeze of lemon juice to taste
Large pinch of black pepper

Put all the ingredients in a food processor or blender and process until smooth. For a spicier mix add a small red chili or a pinch of cayenne pepper. You could also add some fresh coriander and use lime instead of lemon juice; the possibilities are endless!

Lean Bean Curry

228g (8 oz) dried red kidney beans or 2 x 400g (14oz) cans

2 x 400g (14 oz) cans of chopped tomatoes

1 tbsp olive oil

½ tsp cumin seeds

1 large onion chopped

1 deseeded green chili finely chopped

2 cloves of garlic crushed

1 inch of peeled and grated ginger root

1 tbsp curry powder *or*

1 level tsp mild curry paste

1 tsp ground cumin

1 vegetable stock cube

A handful of fresh coriander roughly chopped

Cook the kidney beans according to the instructions or rinse and drain the tinned variety. Heat the oil in a pan and fry the cumin seeds gently for two minutes. Add the onions, chili and garlic and fry for a couple more minutes. Then add the tomatoes, beans, ginger, curry powder or paste, cumin and stock cube and simmer for a further 15 minutes. Towards the end, stir in most of the fresh coriander. Serve with whole grain brown rice and top with natural or Greek yoghurt if desired plus the remaining fresh coriander.

Mmmmm....Meatloaf!

1 pack of turkey bacon (to line tin)

285g (10 oz) lean minced turkey

6 medium egg whites

1 medium onion finely chopped

1 crushed garlic clove

½ tsp paprika powder

1 tbsp Dijon mustard

1 tbsp ketchup

1 vegetable stock cube

1 heaped tbsp chopped fresh basil

A few twists of ground black pepper

1 x 400g (14 oz) tin of chopped
tomatoes (optional)

Preheat the oven to 180 degrees C or 350 F/Gas Mark 4.

Grease and line a non-stick loaf tin with greaseproof paper. Cut the bacon rashers into 3" long strips and line the tin leaving some back. Chop onion and crush the garlic then add all the other ingredients. It's best to squish the mixture with your hands. Pour the mixture into the loaf tin. Cover with remaining bacon and greaseproof paper. Cook for 1 ½ hours. When slightly cooled, slice carefully and serve with a crisp green salad or steamed fresh vegetables. Serves 4 to 6 people, depending how hungry they are!

My Thai Fishcakes

400g (14 oz) can of pink salmon drained (wild Alaskan is best)
113g (4 oz) wholemeal breadcrumbs that have been homemade in a blender

1 medium onion finely chopped

1 vegetable stock cube

3 eggs whites

1 level tsp red curry paste

Juice of half a lemon or lime

Heaped tbsp fresh chopped coriander

Lightly fry the onions in a non-stick pan using a couple of drops of olive oil. Whisk the egg whites until they are creamy and form soft peaks. Drain the salmon thoroughly using a sieve to press out the excess water then mash in a bowl with a fork. Blend the lemon/lime juice with the red curry paste and stock cube and add to the salmon along with the bread crumbs and coriander. Mix in the egg whites using a metal spoon. Cover the bowl with cling wrap and chill for an hour. Scoop out a tablespoonful of the mix and using your hands, form into small rounds. Cook until golden brown in a non-stick frying pan that has been wiped round with a few drops of olive oil. Serve with a colourful mixed salad. This recipe makes about 12 really delicious fishcakes.

Eva's Fruit Cake

340g (12 oz) dried fruit (raisins, chopped apricots, apple, cranberries, cherries, figs etc.)

113g (4 oz) self raising flour (for a wheat-free version substitute rice flour and 2 tsp baking powder)

1 tbsp of sugar replacement granules

1 large cup of cold tea (use a regular tea bag plus a fruit tea bag for extra flavour)

2 egg whites   Grated rind of orange and lemon*

1 tsp mixed spice and 1 tsp cinnamon   3 tbsp ground almonds or chopped nuts*

                                                        Honey to drizzle*   (* All optional)

Soak the fruit in the cold tea overnight. Preheat the oven to 190°C/350°F. Line a loaf tin with greaseproof paper, leaving enough at the sides to fold over the top of cake. Mix the flour, egg whites and spices with the fruit and tea, lifting the mixture high to get air into it. Spoon the mixture into the loaf tin. Sprinkle with ground almonds or chopped nuts and drizzle with honey if using. Cover the top of cake loosely with greaseproof paper and place in the oven for 90 minutes. Uncover for last 20 to 30 minutes of baking.

Pineapple and Cinnamon Drop Scones

113g (4 oz) self raising wholemeal flour plus 113g (4 oz) white self raising flour
or 228g (8 oz) rice flour plus 4 tsp of baking powder for a wheat-free version
1 tsp ground cinnamon
2 egg whites
3 tbsp sugar replacement granules
½ pint pineapple juice
113g (4 oz) semi dried pineapple chopped finely

Pre-heat the griddle (or use a non stick frying pan). Put the wholemeal flour in a bowl and then sieve in the white flour. Add the cinnamon and sugar stir together. Make a well in the middle of the mixture. Add the egg whites and half of the pineapple juice. Blend to a smooth, thick batter. Beat in the remaining juice and chopped pineapple. Wipe the griddle or frying pan with a little olive oil. Set to a low heat. Drop on tablespoons of batter. Leave until bubbles form then turn over and cook on the other side. Serve with a dollop of Greek yoghurt and a drizzle of honey.

10.

Your fantastic potential

your
body knows
best

Being on a journey of discovery, our quest for knowledge is like an insatiable hunger that is never quite satisfied. This hunger is called GROWTH and it is vital for every living being to grow and contribute. Knowledge is like high quality compost that feeds your whole being. The most recent studies show that we only use approximately five percent of our brain. This fact was overwhelming to us! The brain is truly incredible and its capabilities are literally unimaginable. Just think what we would be able to do if we just even tapped into another one or two percent...WOW!

It was during one of our voyages of discovery that we came across the concept of muscle testing. In addition to reading about the subject, we were thrilled to be introduced to one of the few highly qualified musculoskeletal therapists in the UK, a delightful and insightful lady called Marta Abbott. Marta kindly gave us some training and treatment so that we could practice basic muscle testing on ourselves. We were stunned at the accuracy with which Marta determined which areas of our body required treatment owing to certain weaknesses resulting from childhood traumas. She was even able to pinpoint how old we were when these traumas had occurred.

Marta also "communicated" with our body to evaluate the food types that were most appropriate for our individual needs. Fascinating! So, what is muscle testing? Muscle testing, also know as "Applied Kinesiology" is a way of utilising the body to provide feedback on how well we are and on the parts that may require adjustment. A skilled kinesiologist needs a comprehensive knowledge of the skeletal and muscular system. However with a reasonable amount of practice you can learn the basics which will enable you to enrich your life with this awesome technique.

If one touches certain key points of the body and at the same time tests if a certain muscle is weak or strong, this can indicate whether the original key point requires correction. The amazing thing is that muscle testing can identify mental, emotional and physical weaknesses. Using gentle pressure on a certain muscle and then asking the body for an answer, a result can be

216

obtained based upon the strength or weakness of that muscle. Consciously, we often kid ourselves about the state of our well being. However, the body is more likely to give an honest answer by exposing truths that are unknown to the conscious mind. Many different muscles can be tested, but the easiest is generally the deltoid (shoulder) muscle and this is the muscle that we prefer to work with. (For the more experienced, like our new and great friend Marta, there are certain muscles which correspond with specific body parts along the meridian. Meridians are invisible body pathways along which our energy or ch'i flows along according to the principles of traditional Chinese medicine.)

We ask our client to sit down and stretch out their arm to the side at shoulder level. We then apply pressure to their forearm using three fingers while asking the client to resist against it. We watch and feel if the muscle retains its strength or weakens when we ask certain questions. If the muscle stays strong, the body is responding with YES. If the muscle weakens, this means NO. (Several breaks are needed though, as an outstretched arm can become tired).

A great way to try out muscle testing is to practice on a friend or partner. Facing each other, ask your partner to put their left arm out to the side and place their right fist on their stomach. Now whilst holding their right shoulder with your left hand, gently press down on their forearm with your right hand and ask them to resists the pressure. Now ask them to tell you  their name ("My name is..."). If they used their correct name you will find their muscle will stay strong indicating a genuine answer. Now try the same using a fictitious name, for example, "My name is Gongo." You will notice that the muscle will weaken or give way altogether.

This technique is also used to determine whether certain foods and products will elicit an allergic response, have a beneficial effect or just be okay. Here, the product being tested is held against the client's stomach, while their left arm is outstretched so its muscle response can be assessed.

We now practice muscle testing for every new food that we are thinking of introducing into our diet to ensure that we only eat foods that benefit us. Even though we are already aware of which nutrients suit our particular blood group, muscle testing provides a secondary confirmation of which foods are most in tune with our individual needs. So far it has proved to be extremely accurate!

supercharge
your body
with aerobic power!

If you are setting yourself goals for achieving a better life it makes sense that you take a good look at your body. Having a toned, lean and attractive body is not only healthy, it reflects who you are. So it makes to sense to spare some time to work your muscles and get your heart pumping. When you feel fantastic in your own skin it shows.

Our fitness routine starts at 6.00 am every morning. We start by warming up for 15 minutes on our mini trampoline (a small rebounder that you can pick up from all sports equipment stores). This is followed by 30 minutes on the exercise bike using light hand weights and a heart monitor so that we keep within the fat burning zone. We cool down for a further 15 minutes on the trampoline. This equates to one hour of exercise and is followed by some floor work, such as weight lifting and sit ups two or three times a week.

We recommend that beginners start with a five minute warm up, then spend 10 to 15 minutes in the fat burning zone and another five minute cool down. If you don't have hand weights, use two small empty water bottles and gradually increase their weight by adding water. If you don't have a trampoline or bike at home, try warming up and cooling down by marching around your home (or outside) or by stepping up and down the bottom two steps of the stairs.

To get into your fat burning zone you could briskly walk outside or even inside your house, remembering to swing those hips. Or simply use the staircase and walk up and down to music. If you want to be a little more adventurous and enjoy dancing, become your own aerobic instructor and have fun choreographing a 10 to 15

minute dance routine to two or three of your favourite dance tracks. As you get more experienced you can repeat the routine or add more tunes. HAVE FUN! Whatever it takes to get warm and slightly out of breath will help strengthen your heart and take you into the fat burning zone. Making a habit of it will enable you to live a healthier, longer life... Like the famous TV commercial says, JUST DO IT!

Many of our clients think that being fit and healthy means going to the gym, but as you can see, that is not necessary. Gyms and health clubs are great if you enjoy that environment. But if you don't, it is vital you don't create any barriers for yourself. So stay at home and work out your own personal routine. Buy a skipping rope, roller blades or borrow the neighbour's dog and get yourself moving any way you like as long as you do it regularly. You'll soon see and feel the results and look forward to making your muscles work.

Another excuse that we often hear clients say is, "By the time I get home from work I am too tired to exercise or go to the gym." I personally love this excuse as this was the one that Nik and I demolished some years ago! Just GET OUT OF BED EARLIER and work out in the morning before work, before the kids wake up and before you can think of any more excuses! Exercising in the morning has completely revolutionised our life and that of many of our

"Exercise gives your body the juice of life: oxygen. When it wakes up in the morning it thinks 'Yeh! Give me some more of that oxygen because it's just fab!'"

Eva Speakman

clients. If you get your heart pumping and your oxygen in first thing in the morning you have more energy throughout the day and feel an abundance of happiness and a tremendous feeling of achievement. By filling every cell with fresh air and oxygen you can rev your energy levels up to maximum and face the day with more bounce than Tigger!

If you have never been keen on making your body work a bit harder, try it for one day. It's one of the best tonics you can give yourself. Aerobic exercise only needs to be moderately vigorous. You don't have to push yourself to the point of collapse or until the sweat flies off. Just take it steady, make it comfortable and don't forget the warm ups and cool downs, they will make sure you don't ache and feel great.

Exercise burns calories and increases the body's metabolic rate. It decreases the appetite, sharpens the mind, improves your sense of well-being and decreases stress levels. WOW all that and it's totally FREE. If you exercise six times over the next ten days you will see what a REAL difference it makes. It is only by increasing your activity level that you can get your lymph system working better to move toxins out of your body. The lymphatic system is the body's sewage system. Unlike the blood, the lymph does not have a pump (the heart) to push it round the body. It is therefore totally reliant on movement and exercise.

A simple way to get started is to go for a walk and do some deep breathing along the way. Deep breathing exercises will fully oxygenate the blood and it is only with fully oxygenated blood that we can burn fat. Imagine a candle where the wax is our fat. If you put a glass over the candle it goes out. This is why exercise is vital if you are trying to offload some weight.

To remove excess acidity from the tissues you need to build up a reserve of alkalinity through an alkaline diet, including fresh fruit, nuts and green juices. Then this alkalinity must be moved around the body with exercise, massage, yoga or manual lymph drainage. You can keep the body's natural trash clearing system (the lymph) working efficiently by bouncing or dancing yourself fit. Jumping on a rebound mini trampoline can increase lymph flow by 15 to 30 times. Plus it's a great way to feel wide awake in the morning!

"When you **feel good about yourself** you're more **attractive to the world** and more **attractive to success.**"

Eva Speakman

set your
body clock
to live to 100!

The mind is truly fantastic and we often underestimate its capabilities whether it's working on a conscious or sub-conscious level. For example, although most people probably do not realise it, we all have an internal body clock. Some use this clock regularly. In fact, we have had clients tell us that they never need an alarm clock as they naturally wake up at the same time every day. Whereas others struggle to get out of bed!

We are sure that everyone has experienced the situation where they set their alarm clock for a specific time only to wake up five minutes before the alarm goes off. This is a prime example of your internal body clock at work. You can use your internal body clock for all sorts of things and if you tap into it on a regular basis you can even get to the point where you no longer need a watch. Fantastic as this is, it may not be exactly what you want as you may love watches as much as we do!

To prove how in tune I am with my body clock, when Nik and I were blessed with our first little Speakman, Olivia, we were given a due date of 25th December 1996. We were both thrilled with the news. However as it was Nik's birthday on December 7th we both hoped that baby would arrive early so it would be the best possible birthday gift he could imagine!

Throughout my pregnancy, I would tell my lovely bump, "Forget what the doctors say, you're coming into our lives on 7th December." During the final scan Nik asked the medical team, "Is there any chance that this baby will come 2 ½ weeks early?" We were advised that the due date would still be December 25th and that the baby was showing no signs of an early arrival as she was in a breech position and looked to be in no hurry to pop out and shout "WORLD I'M HERE!"

And so December 7th arrived. Despite having no pains or contractions, I was still sure that our baby would be entering the world earlier than everyone else expected to wish her gorgeous daddy a happy birthday. Early that evening, Nik and I set out to meet his parents and cousins at a restaurant for his birthday dinner celebration. As I got into the car with my big bump, my waters broke. Olivia was born on her daddy's birthday at 10.55pm! The entire delivery room cheered and shouted "Happy Birthday!" There wasn't a dry eye in the house!

The medical evidence had confirmed that Olivia would not arrive until the 25th yet my body clock had complied with my personal setting!

You are probably asking why this kind of thing doesn't happen all the time. That's because you haven't yet programmed yourself to make your body clock work properly in the same way you would set your alarm clock. Regrettably, instead of being specific and consistent, most people say to themselves, "I need to get up at 7.00 am or maybe 7.15 am, BUT if I really move fast in the morning, I can sleep in until 7.30 am." This kind of waffle completely confuses the brain and so it virtually ends up saying, "Well if you can't make your mind up, forget it! Go and get yourself an alarm clock!"

Some years ago, Nik and I read a scientific report about a village in Russia where the inhabitants lived to be well over 100 years-old. Scientists studied their lifestyle and diet and took samples of their blood, urine and saliva to ascertain whether there was a genetic explanation for their longevity. Their ultimate conclusion was that the villagers had extended life spans because they woke up naturally each day. They also discovered that a ringing alarm clock is a huge shock to the human body. Brain cells are damaged and even killed as the shock and anxiety unnaturally releases stress chemicals and adrenaline into the bloodstream. Without this daily morning assault on their senses and their simple lifestyle, these Russian villagers were able to live for over 100 years.

So how do you program an internal alarm call? You have to be precise and *specific*. Before going to bed you must decide exactly what time you wish to wake up. You must then look at the time to synchronise your body clock. For example if you go to bed at 11.30 pm you would say, "It is now 11.30 pm. I need to wake up at 7.00 am which gives me 7 ½ hours sleep, no more." Try this out and you will be surprised how quickly you can master the art of body clock control.

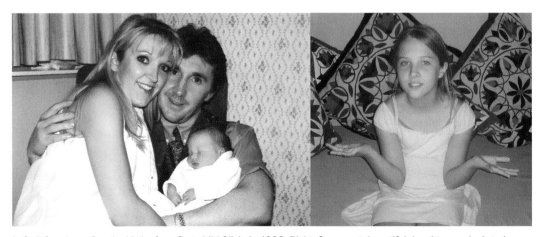

Left: A few days after the birth of our first child Olivia in 1996. Right: Our smart, beautiful daughter as she is today.

perfecting what's on
the **outside**

The bottom line is how you look DOES matter. Research shows attractive people are professionally more successful and have more choice when it comes to selecting a partner. When we say "attractive" we do not necessarily mean that you have to look like a male or female a pin up. Beauty is enhanced by an outgoing, energetic and friendly attitude and a sense that the person has something amazing to offer the world. It is not just about having perfectly symmetrical features and smooth, tanned, skin. Beauty on the outside stems from confidence on the inside.

A positive self-perception, boosted by healthy feedback from others plays a huge role in success. Feeling good about yourself can also become a self-fulfilling prophecy. People who feel they are attractive are perceived to be just as successful as those who are conventionally good looking. So making an effort to look good is not about vanity, it's about being a healthier, more confident and happier person all round. It's about being proud of who you are and realising your full potential. That's why they call it beauty therapy!

We always say if there is something bothering you about your body get it fixed! If your front door needed painting you'd call in the decorators. If your car needed re-spraying you'd drive it to the garage. So why do so many people put themselves at the bottom of the list when it comes to general maintenance? When you've lived with yourself for so long it's easy to get used to having untidy eyebrows, bad teeth or neglected nails for example. Your logical mind tells you these things are not important and your personality is what matters. BUT... your subconscious tells a different story.

Your subconscious controls your body language and that speaks volumes. For example, by putting your hand over your mouth when you smile or continually closing your mouth it shows that you are ashamed of your teeth. Keeping your fists clenched or keeping your hands hidden away in your pockets indicates that you would rather keep them out of sight than inflict their ugliness on the world. A person who is afraid to smile and has lost the use of their hands to express themselves is unable to communicate

as positively and effectively as someone with a fabulous smile and well manicured nails. So two seemingly trivial features can have a very negative impact on how someone feels about themselves, how they portray themselves and how they are perceived.

Having nice teeth will make you feel like smiling much more often and will give you much more confidence. Consider investing in cosmetic dentistry. Today's options include everything from invasive treatments such as implants to replace dentures, to veneers and professional teeth whitening. There are also countless salons offering fast, inexpensive manicures and resin nails which can be decorated with attractive motifs for a bit of extra sparkle. If you have no time for nail salons, set aside some time every few days to clean and file your nails. Men are more likely to nibble them instead of using scissors. This not only looks bad, but it can lead worn down teeth and is totally unhygienic. Come on boys, shape up and file them! It's not girly; it's just an easier way to achieve clean, natural looking well kept hands.

Niggly little things that most of us have, like moles, stretch marks, broken veins, skin tags, grey hair, cellulite, crooked teeth or unwanted hair can all be dealt with safely and effectively by specialists who are dedicated to helping achieve our vision of the body beautiful. Don't be afraid of visiting a beauty salon and asking about their therapies (yes, a lot of men do these days). Even if you only decide to book yourself in for a massage, you are getting yourself acclimatized to looking after yourself and overcoming any self imposed guilt or "I'm not worth it" barriers that have been preventing you from looking and feeling your best.

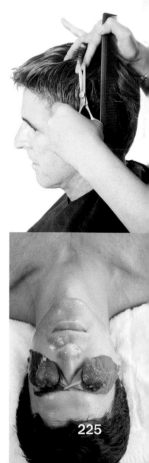

Forget ideas about selfishness or self indulgence. Tell yourself that beauty therapy is just as important to your health as visiting a doctor or seeing an optician, whose job it is to improve the quality of your life. So why not book a day off work and have a pampering day at home. Give yourself a body scrub, put a deep conditioner on your hair, massage your finger and toe cuticles with olive oil, make yourself a face mask of avocado and take a long soak in the bath... mmm, very relaxing.

Spending time on your physical appearance is an investment in your own well-being. It will make you feel cared for, appreciated and valued just like the super special person that you are!

new meaning to "people power"

We have always been interested in human potential and how the mind can make incredible things happen if it focuses on belief. For example, Buddhists believe they can levitate themselves through spiritual meditation, which involves a completely focused state of mind and there are many accounts of this phenomena apparently taking place. While in Africa and South America, there are many records of people lifting themselves, along with other possessions, such as sheep and even cows!

Levitation is also a popular conjuring trick using illusions that are produced by clever mechanics and lighting arrangements. However, that was definitely NOT the case in our experience. If you watched our second series of A LIFE COACH LESS ORDINARY you will have seen us stunned and speechless as we witnessed the most amazing feat of mind power demonstrated by levitation. It was AWESOME in the true sense of the word. It works because of something called "human diamagnetism gravity antenna levitation." No, we don't understand it either!

Apparently, if you get four people together they can create something called a "gravity antenna" which enables them to lift anyone off the ground (no matter how much they weigh). When Nik sat in a chair and was lifted up by the group's fingertips, he seemed virtually weightless as if he was shooting up into the air on his own! Apparently, he could have gone higher, but was limited by the length of our outstretched arms. What he did was imagine he was extremely small and light, like a child. After we had all tuned in to the idea, the impossible became possible. Is this not an analogy for life? Doesn't it just prove that the old saying, "You can do anything when you put your mind to it" is absolutely true.

Fire walking shows how positive thoughts can literally change the body's chemistry and affect how it reacts physically. If you convince yourself you won't get burned then you won't. When Nik and I first tried this we must admit we were quite daunted by the initial thoughts of walking over hot coals that reach a mind boggling 1200F! Yet we managed to get across without a single blister purely by programming our minds to believe that our feet would feel

Fire walking is a tradition in the annual Emperor of the Gods Festival in Malaysia

no pain and would not get burnt. Determination and focus got us safely through this challenge. As in life, success is all about overcoming the negatives by being totally fixed on a positive outcome and ridding yourself of limiting beliefs. For many people the whole experience can be quite spiritual too. You leave your problems at the beginning of the fire and as you walk through you say goodbye to them. Fire walking is a huge metaphor. It says, "After I have walked across that bed of burning embers I will emerge as the person I want to be."

We are all capable of so much more than we believe we are. Sometimes this potential is revealed in extreme circumstances. For example, women have been known to lift up two-ton trucks to free their child who is trapped underneath. Men have brought people safety through burning buildings and raging floods and teenagers have bent steel and ripped open elevator doors to save loved ones. And when told by doctors that they have a terminal illness, people can also heal themselves spontaneously!

When life offers people a choice between their beliefs in what is possible and the worst case scenario, they often get rid of their perceived limitations and do whatever needs to be done. Just think what life would be like if we could just harness this amazing power and heightened awareness all the time instead of just when we are facing a crisis. In the following pages you will read about an incredible man who has done just that and has inspired thousands to go beyond their own self-created limits by abandoning their unfounded fears and imaginary boundaries.

Inspiring lives...

The fire walking challenge reminds us of W. Mitchell, a motivational speaker who most people would consider had experienced a total nightmare of a life. Imagine being consumed by a ball of fire, to lose your hands and your face and end up looking like a cross between Freddie Kruger and Frankenstein. Well, that's what happened to W. Mitchell when he was 28.

W. Mitchell (he prefers to be called Mitchell) was born in the American state of Pennsylvania in 1943. After dropping out of school, serving briefly in the Marines and being a cab driver he worked on the San Francisco cable cars. He was a good looking man with an eye for the ladies and a love of all things mechanical (he liked motorcycles and flying), so the job was a dream come true.

But in July 1971 his life was to change forever. He was on his way to see his girlfriend on his day-old motorcycle, when he was hit by a laundry truck. The lid on the bike's petrol tank came off and gallons of fuel poured all over him and then burst into flames. The inferno was so high it could be seen five streets away. If a passer-by had not put out the blaze with a fire extinguisher Mitchell would have surely died.

Even so, he was barely alive. He had burns to 65% of his body and the doctors thought his chances of survival were slim. His crash helmet saved his scalp, but most of his face and hands were literally burnt off. Fortunately, he had gone into a deep coma and did not endure the agony of the first two weeks. Mitchell did survive (although some might consider he would have been better off dead) and spent months undergoing plastic surgery. Surgeons rebuilt his face as best they could but the results were still far from ideal. His face was a patchwork of grafted skin and he looked so shocking that when he returned to the community a group of children ran away from him screaming, "Monster!"

It was their reaction that encouraged Mitchell to go out and talk about what had happened to him and to show people, especially kids, who he was on the inside. He is a naturally funny man and audiences found his talks both inspiring as well as emotional. As he says, most people have scars that they must deal with although most are invisible, like having abusive parents or dyslexia or some other problem. He encouraged people to learn from someone who had overcome their own more visible scars. By 1987, Mitchell had become a full time motivational speaker, talking at large and small corporate events and charity meetings. His key phrase became "It's not what happens to you in life, it's what you do about it."

Mitchell decided to move from San Francisco because he thought that it would be easier to be known for who he was rather than what he looked like in a small town. So he settled in Crested Butte, a small mining town in Colorado. It was while he was here that his damaged body was to suffer another horrendous injury. Despite losing his hands, Mitchell had continued to train as a pilot and was now able to fly a light aircraft on his own. While taking off with a group of three friends on board, disaster struck again. Unbeknown to him, the wings were covered in a thin sheet of ice, which hampered

the plane's ability to climb.

Seeing rocks ahead, Mitchell stopped the engine so the plane would fall as quickly as possible and it smashed to the ground. All of the passengers escaped unhurt but Mitchell couldn't move and stayed trapped in his seat. After three days in hospital, the neurosurgeon came to tell him that he was paralysed from the waist down and would probably never walk again. Mitchell was devastated. His initial thoughts were that his whole world had suddenly become filled with obstacles and impossibilities. He commented truthfully, "There is probably not one person in a billion who has endured more physical pain than I have."

But gradually one by one, after months of practice in his wheelchair, the obstacles began to disappear and he was able to add another significant message to his motivational speeches: "Before I was paralyzed there were 10,000 things I could do. Now there are 9,000. I can either dwell on the 1,000 I've lost or focus on the 9,000 I have left."

Neither accident has held Mitchell back from living a full and fruitful life. Listing his hobbies as white river rafting and skydiving, he is now a successful businessman, politician, environmental activist

and speaker and travels the world spreading his message of hope: "It's not what happens to you; it's what you do about it." His uplifting philosophy on life is all contained in his book of the same title.

You may be asking, why mention Mitchell in the context of fire walking? A wheelchair-bound burns victim is hardly likely to be anywhere near a bed of red hot coals. Yet fire "walking" was exactly what Mitchell did along with 250 other people at a Tony Robbins seminar. He had only planned to watch, but found himself saying to Tony and another friend, "One of you grab me under the right arm, one under the left, lift me up and turn me around because we are going to do this backwards."

He had more contact with the coals than anyone else as he was literally dragged through them. When he reached the other side there were two dark trails where his feet had been. Yet he did not have a single burn! Mitchell described the experience as a visible illustration of the power people can naturally draw upon when faced with a frightening barrier. It is then that they discover there were no real reason for their fears at all.

> "So many barriers we are told are real, don't exist at all. And even the real ones can be vanquished through sheer effort."
>
> W. Mitchell

> "Your life is entirely what you decide it is. The universe starts in your head and spreads out into the world. Change what happens in your head and the universe changes."
>
> W. Mitchell

"Man in the Mirror"

Michael Jackson

"I'm starting with the man in the mirror
I'm asking him to change his ways
And no message could have been any clearer
If you wanna make the world a better place,
Take a look at yourself and make a change."

This song has great meaning for us and really says what we all should do. Unfortunately most are conditioned to blame others first and to assume there is nothing we can do to change the way we are, or anything around us. When we recognise our true strength and take responsibility for ourselves we can be a powerful force in the world.

I see trees of green...red roses too
I see them bloom...for me and for you
And I think to myself...what a wonderful world.

I see skies of blue...clouds of white
Bright blessed days...dark sacred nights
And I think to myself...what a wonderful world.

And I think to myself...what a wonderful world

Louis Armstrong

"For life to be
fantastic
we need a
fantastic world
to live in."

Eva Speakman

A subject that troubles Nik and I greatly is our failing and fragile world that was once so strong, once so green and pure and once so alive. It has now been proven by scientists that mankind is entirely to blame for this earthly deterioration. It is our responsibility to contribute to reversing and stopping the world from irreparable damage. If we want to continue to see trees of green, red roses and blue skies we need to take action **NOW**.

The only unlimited energy we have is human energy

What is the point of living a fantastic life today if the world we leave behind is in no fit state for our children and their children to enjoy? The earth's natural resources are running out yet demand for them is increasing all the time. By 2030 the world will use at least 40% more oil than it does today. And you must all have heard about global warming and how sea levels will rise and whole countries could disappear from the map. Did you know that the 10 warmest years in history were in the last 14 years?

The main cause of global warming is the burning of fossil fuels. Energy stored over hundreds of millions of years in the form of coal, gas and oil, is being released all of a sudden. When fossil fuels are burned, carbon dioxide (CO_2) goes up into the air and makes a heat-trapping blanket around the planet. The world won't end overnight in 10 years, but a point will be passed where things become impossible to fix.

Feeling and looking fantastic is empowering. So why not use your new energy and vigour to **DO SOMETHING** to make the world a better place for future generations? The world depends on *every individual* to think about what they are doing and consider whether it saps strength from the planet, kills its wildlife or toxifies it in some way. The good life that we can all enjoy today should not be at the expense of our children.

Please think about it. YOU *CAN* MAKE A DIFFERENCE.

Let's all unite to reduce emissions

For those who know Nik and I you may be thinking, "How can you comment on reducing CO_2 emissions with five exotic cars sitting in your garage?" Well that is precisely it! We do have five cars, however they do sit in our garage most of the time. We believe that the average car covers around 12,000 miles a year, whereas we don't even cover anywhere near that annual mileage with all our cars combined. The reason our mileage is so low is because we work from home so we have no regular need to travel. Long distance trips are usually by train. For local trips to the shop, post office, bank, or to feed the ducks, we will usually walk or cycle.

With shopping trips, the secret is to be organised. A standard weekly list will enable you to have just one trip to the supermarket. Olivia goes to school by bus and comes home by car. BUT the school and bus station run is shared with two other families. So instead of three cars on the road, there is only one.

The fact is that pollution from cars is negligible when you consider that the UK's top five polluting companies produce more carbon dioxide emissions than all the vehicles on UK roads put together. But until this situation changes dramatically, it is up to us to help offset the damage.

Regrettably, by far the world's worst polluters are the USA, closely followed by China. Unfortunately, where there is money there is also what appears to be a form of deafness and blindness! It seems that the major decision makers of these countries refuse to see the damage they are causing or hear what the experts and scientists are now urging. There is a saying that "money makes the world go round." However, with this mentality, money will inevitably make the world fall apart.

In the meantime, all of us can make our contribution to helping to cut global warming pollution. Even the smallest measure to saving natural resources and protecting the atmosphere will be appreciated by Mother Earth. We would urge everyone to please join us in our quest to help heal our beautiful and remarkable world by taking some simple actions. These are just a few of the things that we do. We would be so very, very grateful if you would join us.

Help the power stations do less work

Replace old fashioned light bulbs with energy efficient light bulbs.

This is NOT a light bulb...

...it's a HEAT bulb

Now this is a really
cool LIGHT bulb!

Have you ever changed a conventional lightbulb and burnt your fingers? They get incredibly hot. All this heat is made by electricity. Electricity is made by burning fossil fuels. So there's a double problem: you are wasting money paying for needless energy and secondly, carbon dioxide is being pumped into the atmosphere to generate power just to keep your light bulbs scalding hot.

We think the government should let everyone have these free of charge! Not only do they use far less electricity, they last 10 times longer and will save you about £30 over their lifetime. They will also take pressure off the power stations, so they've just got to be worth it. The great news is that these will be the only light bulbs available soon. But why wait? Switch today!

Other things you can do to take the pressure off the power stations

Draft proof your doorways and windows, put a sweater on and turn the thermostat down.

Reduce the temperature of your hot water. What's the point of heating it up to almost boiling just to cool it with the cold tap? Apart from that, scalding water is especially dangerous for children.

Have ONE washing day per week to ensure that your washing machine is always FULL. Don't do lots of half loads.

DON'T USE THE TUMBLE DRYER. If it's a sunny day hang the washing outside.

Unplug electric fires, hair straighteners, the iron, oven etc., the MOMENT you have finished with it.

DON'T leave the refrigerator door open too long.

Replace your old refrigerator, washing machine or dryer with an energy-efficient model.

Turn off the lights when you aren't in a room. Nik always says, "When you leave a room think of the polar bears!" The poor polar bears are going to become extinct as their world is melting away. So when you leave the room, imagine a polar bear stood at the door wagging its finger at you!

Buy products made from recycled materials. Producing paper, glass, and metal products from recycled materials saves 70 to 90% of the energy and pollution that's released when brand new raw materials are used.

236

...and Mother Nature too

Plant a tree! Trees "breathe in" carbon dioxide.

SAVE TREES! Recycling a stack of newspapers only four feet high will save a tree.

Buy products with as little wrapping as possible or with recyclable wrapping.

Reuse or recycle your paper products. When you have papers which are blank on the back, reuse them for notes, colouring sheets, bird cage lining, shopping lists, etc.

Educate everyone to dispose of their recyclable waste. All it takes is a few different coloured bins for cans, glass, paper and plastic and a rota to take the bins to the recycling points.

Clean drinkable water is becoming more scarce. Sweep your driveway instead of hosing it off...share a bath...put half a brick in your cistern tank to reduce the amount of water needed per flush and don't flush unless you've left a deposit!

Don't use chemical fertilisers, herbicides, or pesticides on your lawn or garden. Pesticides don't just kill bad insects, they also kill beneficial insects and wildlife and create health problems for humans.

Use environmentally friendly cleaning products around the house.

To find out more about the fragile condition of the planet and why we must ALL act now, we recommend you watch *An Inconvenient Truth* by Al Gore or buy his thought provoking book.

> "It's obvious that every man, woman and child can contribute to the well being of our native wildlife and the planet through simple day-to-day stuff such as recycling, chemical and pollution awareness, and not wasting water."
>
> Steve Irwin

Let's all work together on this one
for our children and their children.
LET'S SAVE THE EARTH!

On behalf of the planet and our children, thank you!

Inspiring lives...

One of our goals that will now remain unticked was to meet the late great Steve Irwin. We can only think that this wildlife warrior had concluded his job here; he had shown us all what to do and he is now allowing us all to take over as he is needed elsewhere. The world without doubt has lost the most remarkable spokesperson for animals that constantly fear for their lives because of the perception that as Steve said, "Snakes were something you hit with a stick. Crocodiles were evil ugly monsters and koalas and kangaroos made great fur coats."

Steve opened our eyes to what animals were having to endure and also to what could be done to protect them. (That is why we are donating part of the proceeds from the sale of this book to Conservation Worldwide, which is supported by Chester Zoo, where my own boyhood dreams of working with animals began. Until we can do more personally, this will be part of our contribution for now. Also, by giving monies freely to charity we know that our generosity will always find its way back to us as this is one of the first laws of spiritual success and is another great reason to contribute to organisations that rely on donations.)

The Australia Zoo was originally a small reptile sanctuary founded by Steve's father, so Steve literally grew up with kangaroos, possums, crocodiles and snakes as they were in and around his house! After leaving school, he followed in his father's footsteps and worked (for no pay) as a crocodile rescuer capturing wild crocodiles that were considered a danger and taking them to his father's sanctuary. Keen to share his experiences, he set up an old video camera in a tree. He then showed the film to a TV producer friend who insisted that he made a TV documentary. Following in the footsteps of his hero David Attenborough, Steve set out to educate the world, explaining, "Crocodiles do not make good pets but I find them endearing, modern day dinosaurs still here: 22 odd species, 16 of them endangered."

The Crocodile Hunter showed him wrestling with reptiles and tackling deadly snakes. Steve's whacky style, boundless energy and his habit of shouting "Crickey!" captivated viewers everywhere. People who have met him say he was the same over the top, extrovert person off camera as he was on it! As his agent, Anthony Field said, "He was Mr Enthusiasm, exactly like he was on TV. He was an honest, hard-working guy who loved his family, loved wildlife and he really was dedicated to bringing the love of wildlife to children, to adults...to everybody." Over 70 episodes of *The Crocodile Hunter* were made, which have reached over five hundred million viewers in more than 200 countries.

Steve first saw his American wife-to-be Terri, while he was giving a crocodile demonstration at his zoo in 1991. He described the moment saying, "I had this 15 foot croc. I'm feeding him and you can see how beautiful he is...and I look up and there's this woman in the crowd and our eyes meet, and I'm like, [gasp]. Dead-set, love at 20 feet. She's drop dead gorgeous and I'm spellbound; shot in the heart with cupid's arrow. Wow!" They married a year later.

Terri, who ran her own wildlife sanctuary, shares Steve's passion for wildlife and they even spent part of their honeymoon filming the first episode of *The Crocodile Hunter*. (To celebrate their tenth wedding anniversary they went to Indonesia to help out at an elephant sanctuary!) Four years later, they had a daughter who they named Bindi (after Steve's favourite crocodile!) and then a son Robert.

Steve's enormous media profile attracted huge numbers of visitors to the zoo and he used this as a means to save more animals rather than to raise his own standard of living. His family remained in the modest bungalow his dad built on the zoo's grounds in the 1970s. For Steve, fame was an open door to educate the world about something he adored: all creatures great and small. In fact, virtually every single cent that he made from *The Crocodile Hunter* and other TV and movie appearances has been ploughed straight back into conservation and into acquiring land in Africa, Fiji and the United States. Being especially worried about the thousands of acres being cleared for farming and urban building, he said in an interview, "Whenever we get enough cash and see a chunk of land we're passionate about, bang, we buy it."

In 2000, Steve's mother was tragically killed in a car crash. In honour of her memory Steve set up the Lyn Irwin Memorial Fund with proceeds going to the Australian

"I'm a wildlife warrior. A warrior is someone who is trained or engaged in battle. My battle is conservation... My mission is to educate people about conservation... Come with me. Shaaaare it with me. Share my wildlife with me. Because humans want to save things that they love."

Steve Irwin

Wildlife Hospital which cares for sick, injured and orphaned koalas and other native wildlife before releasing them back into the wild. In 2002, Steve also founded Wildlife Warriors Worldwide Ltd for the protection of injured, threatened or endangered animals.

To Steve the facts were blindingly clear. As the biggest trade second only to the pharmaceutical industry, wild animals across the globe are being slaughtered mercilessly and have no chance unless humans intervene. As he said, "I believe that the time has come where if we don't get animals into people's hearts, they're going to go extinct... 90% of our fish are being lost; our great apes are being caught up in the bush meat industry and their habitats are being destroyed. They're caught in a war. They've got AIDS. It's like they are dying. Our animals are dying at such a great rate..."

In September 2006, Steve was at the Great Barrier Reef being filmed for a new children's show that he was doing with his daughter. He was snorkelling over the top of a stingray that was buried in the sand. Because a photographer was blocking its getaway, the fish felt threatened and threw up its barbed tail which hit Steve in the chest and went directly into his heart. Stunned, as we were, by the news of his sudden death, people around the world flooded his zoo with flowers and notes. An incredible 360 million people tuned in to watch his memorial service.

Because of his passion to help the world's animals, Steve Irwin did not die a rich man. Whether it was the threatened extinction of tigers in India, freshwater dolphins in China, the elephants in Africa or the horrors of commercial whaling, Steve worked tirelessly to help save them by bringing their plight to the world's attention. For example, when rare birds and other creatures were threatened by a dam that was being built in Belize, he flew out with a camera crew and made a TV programme to save them. He was very last hope for helpless rare and endangered animals all over the world.

Now he is gone, it is up to us all to learn from his teachings, follow his example and continue with his legacy. The Australia Zoo was Steve's vision of paradise and we hope that you will join us in contributing to his crusade to save what remains of our planet's beautiful but fast disappearing wildlife.

To make a donation visit:
http://www.wildlifewarriors.org.au/

All the administration costs for the Wildlife Warriors charity are covered by the Australia Zoo so that 100% of donations can be used directly for wildlife conservation.

Be a "wildlife aware" consumer

Trade in wildlife is driven by consumer demand. So when the buying stops the death and destruction will too. Even today, the luxury fashion magazines are still featuring "exotic skin" accessories and clothes made from lizard, snake, alligator, crocodile and even stingray skin. Check to see if the product is "faux" which means it is a realistic manmade version. Otherwise don't buy anything that is made with wild or exotic animal skin or other body parts.

Chinese medicines containing tiger bone, rhino horn or bear bile and anything made using natural fur or elephant ivory are other products to be avoided completely. Say "NO" too to shark fin soup, anything made from turtle shells, coral, sponges, sea shells or dried seahorses. Check before you buy products made from rosewood, mahogany, cypress, ebony or teak. (Of a shipment of mahogany from the rainforest, it is alleged that just 3% will have been legally chopped and exported.) Make sure you buy only from an environmentally aware supplier of "certified sustainable" wood products. For more details visit:
http://www.traffic.org/help/guide.htm

"I have no fear of losing my life. If I have to save a koala or a crocodile or a kangaroo or a snake... I will save it."

Steve Irwin

Epilogue

Are the Speakmans deluded? Are they living in the real world? Do they ever watch the news? We hear this kind of thing all the time. Of course we know what's happening and there's plenty of bad news out there. People are being killed, the planet is overheating and according to which experts you believe, we are all going to be wiped out by bird flu, germ warfare, flooding or starvation depending on which global catastrophe comes first. Plus, we are just like everyone else; things go wrong. Life isn't always going to run smoothly, but it's how you perceive things that matters.

How is feeling miserable and defeated going to help? The fact there is so much adversity around us makes it even more important to focus on the positives in order to deal with the negatives. It is a well known fact that you can't help anyone until you've helped yourself. Remember the video they play before you take off in an airplane? You need to put your own oxygen mask on before you can help anyone else. There's a good reason for this. If you run out of air you won't be capable of saving anyone else's life and certainly not your own. Negatively programmed people who focus on their own worries, frustrations and cravings are more likely to look at an upsetting situation in the world and say there is nothing they can do about it. Plus they are in need of sympathy and attention themselves. When they are positively programmed and free from constant introspection and self analysis they are in a better position to help others and to be valued and loved. Eva and I have discovered that this is where the path to true happiness lies.

No one is guaranteed a long and thriving life. We are only guaranteed one moment at a time. So really make the most of those moments and don't cheat yourself with half measures. Put your heart into everything you do. Give your children your undivided attention when they talk to you. Complete every job to the best of your ability. Show your loved ones you love them. When exercising give it your all. Share your positivity and passion with others. Make every moment special. Make special moments happen! As Mahatma Gandhi said, "You must BE the change you wish to see in the world." It takes courage to change things and face your fears. But once you do you will progress like you never have before. You will experience things you never thought possible and you will start living your dreams. Your work and home environments will become more harmonious and you will encourage more joy into your life.

For us, there is absolutely no such thing as a bad day! Every day is FANTASTIC, even if it's raining! Too many of us have fallen into the trap of expecting the worst out of everything and everyone. But you have the power to adjust your default settings. YOU CAN DECIDE HOW YOU WANT THINGS TO BE. Please remember that YOU and only YOU are the source of ALL your emotions. Nothing and no one can change how you feel, except you. If you find yourself reacting to anything, once you realise what is really happening you can change it in a moment!

Quantum physics teaches us that our physical reality is mouldable and this truth excites us. It means we can create whatever we want if we work with the quantum laws. Our thoughts shape the universe and the matter we see. Quantum research even proves that particles of light and matter behave differently when we watch them! As we know, three people witnessing a car crash will see three different things. So we co-create our physical universe via the power of our minds making up what become "holographic creations" made from waves of sound and light.

As energy follows thought, thought is the essence of power and focused thought becomes *focused power*. Much of the thought that creates our world is weak, scattered and unfocused. With practice, you can learn to focus your mind's power and create the reality you want and deserve. The laws of quantum physics show that everything must be created first in our own inner world. Our inner reality then becomes our blueprint and then physical matter is attracted to this "template" by the laws of quantum attraction. This is how the world you see comes into existence!

So as you finish this first step of your journey with us, we would like to compliment you for your dedication in following through and reading our book to the end. There is no success in life without investment and well done you for making that investment. We sincerely hope that you are able to see, feel and hear changes in your life already and we want you to know that just like us, you need to practice every day so that some of the life changing skills that we have shared with you become part of your unconscious competence and the others, such as your WOW list will form part of your daily ritual.

Practice is very important. Remember the first time you tried to ride a bike or tried to tie your shoelaces? Difficult! Yet you don't give either of these actions a second thought now. You really need to take *daily action* to propel yourself towards your real life's purpose. We cannot express how important this is. After all you wouldn't go to the gym and exercise like mad for a week and then say that's it; I am fit for life! So we now want to challenge you seven more times with some reminders as follows:

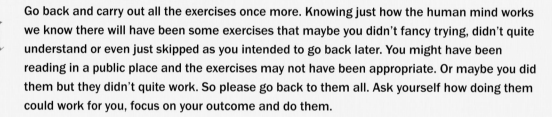

1 Go back and carry out all the exercises once more. Knowing just how the human mind works we know there will have been some exercises that maybe you didn't fancy trying, didn't quite understand or even just skipped as you intended to go back later. You might have been reading in a public place and the exercises may not have been appropriate. Or maybe you did them but they didn't quite work. So please go back to them all. Ask yourself how doing them could work for you, focus on your outcome and do them.

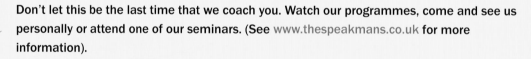

2 Don't let this be the last time that we coach you. Watch our programmes, come and see us personally or attend one of our seminars. (See www.thespeakmans.co.uk for more information).

3 Take the four main goals that you must achieve within the next year. Write them down again separately from the rest and then underneath each one write a huge paragraph stating why you *absolutely must* achieve that goal within the next year. Explain exactly why you must achieve it and what it will do for you. Imagine what life will look like when you have reached your goal. Feel how good it is to know you have been successful and hear the voice in your head telling you just how fantastic you are. So develop a plan for each goal. Break the goal down into manageable steps and then take the first action towards each step and start the ball rolling. That could be a phone call, gathering information from the Internet or telling someone all about what you are going to do.

We do hope that we will have the opportunity to meet you one day and to hear your story, as we confidently know that if you follow our guidance within the pages of this book that *YOUR* LIFE CAN BE FANTASTIC TOO!

We wish you the best possible future filled with happiness, success and fulfillment.

Love and hugs,

Nik and Eva

 Continue reading your WOW lists daily and feeling those fantastic feelings that are associated with the major achievement in your life so far. Your WOW list is a continuous document that you will be able to increase. And we can assure you that you will soon be extending it with many wonderful new additions as your life changes.

 Remember to take stock of your achievements. Look back at what you wrote at the beginning of this book. Give yourself credit for the progress you have already made and learn to put things clearly into perspective. Accept that your progression so far is only the *start* of your journey to a new and fantastic life.

 Remember, that you are a one-off! There is no one else on this planet that looks or acts like you. You personality is unique and as such you can shape and mould it in any way you choose. Take a look in the mirror straight into your own eyes and compliment yourself for being a unique human being. Tell yourself about your plans and get yourself excited about your truly remarkable and fantastic life.

 Accept that this book finishes but that it is most definitely not the end but the beginning; the beginning of your new life, the life that you always wanted and thoroughly deserve.

And finally... some more words from the successfully Speakmanned

Theresa

On my first visit to the Speakmans I was ashamed and very nervous but I instantly felt at ease with Nik. He made me feel comfortable and special and in no time I was blurting out thoughts I would not have told my family. Nik has a true gift in making people feel normal and at ease.

He made me realise that I do matter and that I must save myself first. I suddenly felt that I deserved to look and feel my best and the following day I made an effort with my appearance. I have since made some drastic changes to myself physically and feel utterly fantastic. I feel strong, I feel young and I feel vibrant. For the first time in my life I know exactly what I want and I am getting it!

After being a gambling addict for many years, I no longer spare slot machines a single thought. Nik cured me of this addiction and I am so grateful that he cleared away the cobwebs that were stopping me from seeing what I really wanted. My whole life has changed and my focus has changed. I look decades younger and even have a partner who is 20 years my junior! Truly magnificent!

Angela

I just want to say well done back to you for all the lives you have changed. That's more Godly in my eyes than most Churches manage to achieve in this day and age... I am Catholic and believe in many things especially Christianity but see so little of it in my day to day life. It costs nothing to smile at a stranger but its impact can be life changing...

Craig Price

Since our meeting I found you both to be exactly what I expected you to be (awesome). Working with you both has been an incredible experience, one I wish for anyone looking to enrich any or all areas of their life.

Annemarie Dalley

Nik and Eva, In a world where it seems cool to be cynical you are like a breath of fresh air. You guys have had such a big effect on me. Thank you!

Jane

Many, many thanks for yesterday. I know you also spent so much extra time with me but didn't realise just how much until I was leaving and glanced at my car clock! Thank you. I felt very tired by the time I returned home but today feel really good. I awoke feeling very positive and very much "lighter." I was quite nervous about coming to see you, but you welcomed me into your home and family as if I was a member of it, if that makes any sense.

I know you are both younger than I, but you are the sort of "parents" that most people can only dream about. You told me straight but then guided me along the way and wouldn't let me off the hook, unconditional love and genuine concern. I took a look at you both with your beautiful children standing on the porch, waving me off and this lovely warmth emanated through to my soul. You greeted me with very open hearts and that is the very secret of great therapists. Thank you. I'm now just about to go into the kitchen and remove all the stuff I shouldn't eat and throw it away!!!!!!! Bless you.

Julie

Thank you SO MUCH for taking the time to contact me and again, your timing is spookily appropriate! I have been hauling myself back on the wagon (rather more slowly than I had hoped) and just today managed to jump properly on board. I think I was just exhausted and needed to relax a little but hey I'M BACK! Friends are starting to notice differences in me, not just in size but in attitude. They can't actually believe the willpower that I have (well it has evaded me for 47 years!) and I can't believe that you accomplished that in just a few hours! THANK YOU!!!

Thanks again for the support it REALLY helps. It also amazes me that you find the time between books, TV, work and life. You are both a real inspiration!

Donna

The Speakmans have helped me to become a more positive, friendly and outgoing person who now wants to live life to the full. Before I met them I was a very negative person who could not discuss my feelings or so-called problems without wanting to cry. By talking to me and helping me understand the way the mind works, I understood that what we say and how we think can determine how we feel. I no longer dwell on past events which were making me unhappy. I now know that although we cannot change these events we can focus on the tasks of the future and give ourselves a life to look forward to.

I now have ambitions and goals in my life. The Speakmans have helped me to get to this point by guiding me to understand that is up to me how I feel and how I live my life and NOT up to other people. I made notes before my sessions on what and what I had accomplished as well as issues that needed to be discussed. At first, writing things down was difficult because it made them seem real. But eventually this became easier because I began to feel I could cope with most areas of my life, because for the first time, I was in control.

Angela Webster

I work in the medical profession and I do understand that people who are ill are on a low ebb but you Speakmans should be available on prescription. Keep doing what you are doing you're an inspiration!

Dr J. Bradley

Nik and Eva, thanks to your programme and especially your attitude, (which is fantastic) I've got my "get up and go" and dumped my rear view mirror to really move ahead with my coaching practice. Seeing you apply hypnotherapy and NLP with such great compassion and to such great effect has proven to me that I can really help people too!

Viv Connor

I Just wanted to say that all my husband and I say is the word FANTASTIC. It makes us feel great and starts the day well. You talk about finding someone who has done the thing that you want to achieve and model them; well you two are our models.

Michelle

I have so many people asking if you are really that nice, I tell them that TV does not do you any justice you are earth angels.

Andy Graham

Just wanted to let you know I have really enjoyed your shows and, just by watching you on the TV you have somehow reminded me that there are some super human beings out there!

Vishal Passan

Hi Nik, I just wanted to say how fascinated I was watching your programme. I think Eva and yourself do a fantastic job.

Shirley Bradfield

I have found you both so inspiring and kept the programmes and are re-watching them for inspiration and have found so many points that have helped to get me through the REALLY BAD TIMES.

Maria Barton

You are so radiant and believe that everything is possible. I don't think many life coaches would believe and would be able to do some of the things you do.

Paul Ribbons

Thanks to the Dream Catchers I am free to catch mine and that makes me feel fantastic. The Speakmans have without exception the best job in the world. And they happen to be awesome at it!

Michelle

I know you probably won't remember me but I have spoken to you a few times on Key 103. I was the one with the fear or dogs. And I would just like to say thank you because my fears have now all gone including the spider one. Thank you again. You have changed my life around just by listening to you on Late Night Nicksy.

Paul Field

Thank you, for changing my life!

Acknowledgments

"If I can see farther then anyone else, it is because I stand on the shoulders of giants!"

Mark Twain

We would like to send the greatest, hugest, most enormous thanks to Julia Kantecki, who having seen our way of life concluded there was just no other way to live. She then tirelessly studied, listened and did everything possible to help us to write this book. Julia is a true example of our statement that ANYTHING IS POSSIBLE, she is an IGNITER and a friend for life.

Thanks to Sue Rider our strict, hard working and very wise agent. Thanks also to Rob Hallam for producing our very first showreel and a very big thanks to Paul Coleman, the production team and everyone at UKTV for believing in us and helping us to get our message to a wider audience well within our goal time frames. Your support has helped us to help more people realise that their lives really can be FANTASTIC!

Our heartfelt appreciation also goes to Janet Scott for looking after our children so well, thus enabling us to continue with our life mission, and to Olivia and Hunter for their patience and understanding and for playing so nicely while mummy and daddy were typing so excitedly on their computers working to conclude this book.

Thanks to all the inspirational people mentioned in this book for having had such a tremendous influence in our life and also to all the other inspiring people out there, that like us, are making their contribution to change the world for the better.

Finally, to all our clients past, present and future for gifting us with the best job in the world. It is a true privilege and honour to introduce you all to your own fantastic lives.

"Thank you!"

There are four groups of people who impact
our path of life:
Those who merely cross it, and pass by,
Those who try to trip you and make you fall,
Those who walk with you
And those who carry you in times of weakness
until you gain strength.
To all those people, past and present, good and bad,
we thank you all.
For it is you that have made us the incredible
and fantastic people we are today.

Eva Speakman

10 Speakman Beliefs

1. We believe *anything* is possible.

2. We believe if you give, you will receive.
If you give love, you will receive love...
if you give kindness, you'll receive kindness...

3. We believe you should never intentionally
harm another living being.

4. We believe that our children are the future,
and so should be nurtured, guided, loved and respected.

5. We believe it is disrespectful to yourself and your body
to chemically impair your state through
drugs, alcohol or tobacco.

6. We believe you should surround yourself
with people who support your aspirations.

7. We believe in having clear goals.

8. We believe in ourselves and each other.

9. We believe in offering our help to those who need it.

10. We believe in you!

The publisher would like to thank the following for their kind permission to reproduce their photographs:

Les and Renate Pearce
http://www.studiofirst.co.uk/

Jim Marks Photography
http://www.marks.co.uk

Harrison Funk
http://www.proud.co.uk

Marc Pagani
http://www.marcpagani.com

Carl W. Southerland
http://www.betterphoto.com/gallery

Illustration on p.121 by Dominic Murphy
http://www.dominicmurphyart.com

All other images used under license from:

Shutterstock Inc
155 W. 19th St., 2nd Floor
New York
NY 10011, USA
http://www.shutterstock.com

BigStockPhoto.com
2919 Bellows Ct
Davis
CA 95616, USA
http://www.bigstockphoto.com

Photorazzi.com
Photorazzi, LLC
4521 PGA Blvd. Suite 336
Palm Beach Gardens
FL 33418, USA
http://www.photorazzi.com

White House Archive (Bush Library) 1990
Additional images © Goldwing Publishing Ltd